IMAGES
of America

MADURA'S DANCELAND

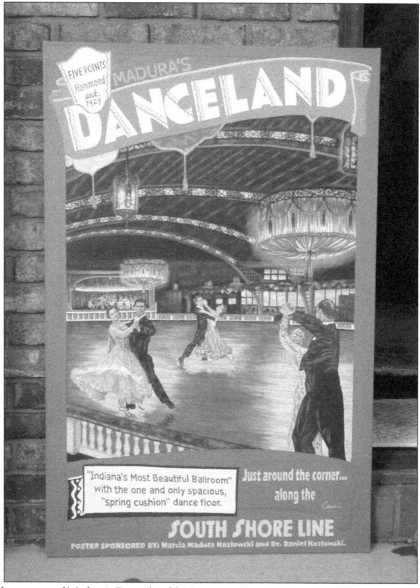

This oil painting of Madura's Danceland by Hammond artist Bruce Cegur was commissioned by Marcia Madura Kozlowski and Dr. Daniel R. Kozlowski as part of the South Shore Line poster series of the Northwest Indiana Forum. Cegur worked from two black-and-white photographs of the Danceland interior and from personal memories. "Marcia told me everything she remembered—the colors, the fabrics, the way things glowed—and I tried to make it happen," Cegur said. The poster unveiling ceremony took place on May 18, 2003, at the legendary Phil Smidt and Son Restaurant, which was located on the north end of Calumet Avenue in Hammond near where Danceland had stood for 38 years. (Courtesy of Bruce Cegur; photograph by Dr. Daniel R. Kozlowski.)

ON THE COVER: This 1929 photograph of Madura's Danceland features the Dance Instructor's Club, directed by Eugene Leinen, on the famous maple wood dance floor. The 10-piece band of Jimmy Kirkwood and the Campus Serenaders is on stage. Owner Michael Madura Sr. is seated in the second row, fourth from the right. (Courtesy of the estate of Evelyn Madura Halik.)

IMAGES
of America

MADURA'S DANCELAND

Patrice Madura Ward-Steinman

ARCADIA
PUBLISHING

Published by Arcadia Publishing
Charleston SC, Chicago IL, Portsmouth NH, San Francisco
CA

Library of Congress Control Number: 2009943865

For all general information contact Arcadia Publishing at:
Telephone 843-853-2070
Fax 843-853-0044
E-mail sales@arcadiapublishing.com
For customer service and orders:
Toll-Free 1-888-313-2665

Visit us on the Internet at www.arcadiapublishing.com

*To the memory of my father, Michael J. Madura Jr.,
who preserved and documented the colorful history of
Danceland so that it would never be forgotten*

CONTENTS

ACKNOWLEDGMENTS

Unless otherwise noted, all of the images appearing in this book are a part of the Madura archive, primarily of my late father, Michael J. Madura Jr. He organized, preserved, and labeled more than 50 years of official documents, wrote extensive personal memoirs of the business, and photographed both the inside and outside of Danceland, complete with descriptive titles. Without his collection, this book would not have been possible.

Great appreciation for additional photographs, memorabilia, and historical facts is due, especially, to my siblings Marcia (and Daniel) Kozlowski and Michael D. (and Charlene) Madura; to my aunts Evelyn Halik (deceased) and Doris Borg and to their daughters Bonnie Kekelik, Patti Pemberton, Lynn Massey, and Diane Richardson; and to the entire Madura extended family of generations past and present for their work at Danceland, especially to my late mother, Henrietta, and grandmother Julia for marrying the two unique men who made Danceland a legend, Michael J. Madura Sr. and Michael J. Madura Jr.

Additional thanks are due to Stephen G. McShane, archivist/curator of the Calumet Regional Archives at Indiana University Northwest; to Gayle Faulkner Kosalko, editor of the Whiting-Robertsdale newspaper, *WRite Stuff*; to artist Bruce Cegur (www.cegur.com); and to John and Jana Higgerson for their photographs and perspectives on being a rock musician at Danceland in the 1960s.

This book would never have happened without the inspiration of screenwriter June August, who first saw the potential of a dramatic story and asked me to begin interviewing the Maduras for their memories; of author and historian Michael L. Mark, who insisted that the Danceland archive was a "gold mine" for a historical study and prodded me year after year to complete this book; and of my husband, composer and professor David Ward-Steinman, whose wellspring of love, support, knowledge, enthusiasm, and generosity is boundless and beyond my wildest dreams.

I also wish to thank Anna Wilson, the acquisitions editor at Arcadia Publishing, for her gracious acceptance of the proposal and gentle encouragement during the publishing process. I am eternally grateful to her, to John Pearson, the Midwest publisher at Arcadia, to Rob Kangas, the Midwest production coordinator at Arcadia, and to the reviewers for believing in the richness of our story.

INTRODUCTION

Danceland! Just the name conjures up memories of dancing and romancing to thousands of live big bands for hundreds of thousands of couples from all around the Calumet Region of Northwest Indiana and Chicago's East Side. Opening night in October 1929 drew over 2,000 people to the beautiful ballroom with the famous maple wood dance floor. It continued to thrive with live music three to four nights a week, 12 months a year, throughout the big band era despite the Great Depression, and World War II and beyond, until it burned to the ground on Sunday morning, July 23, 1967. Almost everyone's marriage in "the Region" began as a dance at Madura's Danceland. In the 38 years Danceland was open, it had only two owners and managers, father and son Michael J. (Mike) Madura Sr. and Michael J. (Mick) Madura Jr. It remained a family business for all those years, with four generations of the Madura family having worked there in many capacities.

Madura's Danceland was located at Five Points, which is the five-starred intersection in Whiting/Robertsdale where Indianapolis Boulevard, Calumet Avenue, and 114th Street all intersect at the gateway to Lake Michigan and Chicago. Visitors to this highly industrialized area today would find it difficult to believe that just 200 years ago the area was comprised of lush forests and wetlands where the Potawatomi Indians lived, hunted, fished, and farmed. Kenneth Schoon, in his book *Calumet Beginnings*, explains it is unique in that it is a headwaters region with the Eastern Continental Divide running through it, so that all streams begin there and run either north or south. The Potawatomi began to lose their self-sufficiency when they engaged in fur trading with French explorers and trappers in the 1700s. When Indiana and Illinois became states in 1816 and 1818, respectively, and Chicago became an incorporated town in 1833, the Potawatomi were forced to relinquish their homeland in the Calumet Region and slowly trek westward to Kansas.

The first settlers to the Hammond and Whiting areas arrived from Germany in 1847, and by 1851 the Michigan Southern and Northern Indiana Railroad line was built. George M. Roberts, a hunter from Pennsylvania, purchased 470 acres, including Lake Michigan frontage, to be used primarily for farming animals. When he donated a right-of-way across his land to the Pennsylvania Railroad in 1858, the area was called Robertsdale in his honor. In 1897, Hammond annexed Robertsdale and Roby, the northern strip of land between the Illinois state line and Whiting (although people from this area have always had Whiting mailing addresses and phone numbers).

Three railroad lines were built parallel to each other along the Lake Michigan shore: the Michigan Southern and Northern Indiana Railroad, the Pennsylvania Railroad, and the Baltimore and Ohio ("the B and O"). The once heavily forested area gave way to industry, which in Hammond included a meatpacking plant, a lumberyard, a sawmill, and a planing mill. In 1889, the Standard Oil Company established its refinery, the largest in the world at that time, in Whiting. Other Calumet Region heavy industries included the largest railroad passenger car manufacturing plant in the country (the Pullman Company), the largest commercial limestone quarry (Thornton), the largest steel mill in the world (U.S. Steel's Gary Works), the world's largest cement plant (Universal Portland Cement), and the 100-acre Amaizo plant in Roby, which made corn products.

The industrial might of the Calumet Region and Chicago brought tens of thousands of immigrants from Germany, Czechoslovakia, Poland, Croatia, Ireland, Lithuania, Sweden, England, Wales, Scotland, Canada, Italy, and Serbia to the area during the 1900s. By 1910, some 78 percent of Chicago's residents were immigrants or the children of immigrants. From 1916 through the 1920s, more than 75,000 African Americans traveled north via the Illinois Central Railroad to the South Side of Chicago. The Great Migration included many musicians, including Erskine Tate, Jelly Roll Morton and Joe "King" Oliver.

Whiting/Robertsdale became a close-knit community of religious people who attended six different Roman Catholic churches, nine Protestant churches, and a synagogue, each serving a particular ethnic group. Whiting/Robertsdale's population was 90 percent Slavic, and 50 percent of that was specifically Slovak. While the large number of immigrants working hard labor might suggest that illiteracy was prevalent, Archibald McKinley, in his book *Oil and Water: A Pictorial History of Whiting/Robertsdale, Indiana*, states that because of Standard Oil's emphasis on scientific laboratories, Whiting/Robertsdale had the highest per capita number of Ph.D.s of any community in Indiana.

The population explosion in the area and the rigors of hard labor created a demand for recreation and relaxation, and amusement parks, skating rinks, public theaters, movie houses, ice cream parlors, poolrooms, penny arcades, and dance halls sprang up in and around Chicago. One such place was the famous Five Points in the Calumet Region, the gateway to Chicago along the Lake Michigan shore, which was famous as an amusement destination for Chicagoans and Hoosiers. The town of Roby, sandwiched along a 1-mile stretch of Indianapolis Boulevard between the Five Points intersection and the Illinois state line, has a colorful history that began as a haven for Chicago criminals. A few notable ones organized a gambling casino where bets were made over dice, cards, horse racing, motor racing, dog racing, and boxing, with other vices available as well. The Indianapolis government tried to control the activities, but the physical isolation of the Calumet Region from the rest of Indiana made constant control impossible. Eventually the Roby Speedway became independent, attracted thousands of spectators weekly, and spawned many famous drivers, including George Souders, who became a national hero by winning the Indianapolis 500 in 1927.

All of this entertainment was easily accessible via trolley cars as early as 1894. The trolleys provided inexpensive transportation to Five Points, and a miniature tram sponsored by Hammond mayor Charles O. Schonert transported people from the trolleys to the beautiful Hammond Beach Inn and Zoo at Lake Michigan, to the fish houses (and to their annexes, which supplied Prohibition-era libations), to the Whiting Friars Ballpark, and to the Indiana Gardens Roller Rink. Before the massive Lever Brothers' soap factory was built on the most prominent "point" at Five Points, that lot was a vacant field used in the autumn for football games and in the summer for touring carnivals. What a lively and interesting place Five Points was! Michael J. Madura Jr. once wrote:

> Standing on the corner of Five Points near Hammond Beach, the train whistle blows, reminding us of the fabled playground the area once was. Flashbacks reel through our minds like movies: Roller Coasters to Roller Skating . . . Dining and Dancing to Midnight Romancing . . . Carnival Games to Big Band Names . . . Ice Cream and Custard to Hot Dogs and Mustard. Throngs came from miles around to taste the sweet nectars of the region's cornucopia.

One

INDIANA GARDENS

Madura's Danceland wasn't even a gleam in 21-year-old Mike Madura's eye back in 1909, when he first ventured into business as a roller-skating instructor and later as manager of the Whiting Roller Rink, located at 1865 Indianapolis Boulevard and owned by Herman Vater. It was there that Mike Madura first met his redheaded Irish sweetheart, 19-year-old Julia Cannon. They were married at Sacred Heart Church in Whiting on September 11, 1911, and then came three children, Michael J. (b. 1912), Evelyn (b. 1914), and Doris (b. 1920), all of whom became integral to the operation of Danceland.

Mike Madura's expertise as a roller skater, skating instructor, and organizer of a skating basketball team attracted the public from around the Calumet Region and later gained him recognition in the *Spink Sport Stories*. Business boomed at the Whiting Roller Rink, and on December 6, 1916, Madura and partner Julius Linnemann leased a new park development at the southwest corner of Five Points and had the lessors John and Charles Varellas and Andrew Stergios build the "largest rink in the state of Indiana" on it. The new rink, bandstand, checkroom, and lunch bar were built in a woodland clearing on the shores of Wolf Lake. Linnemann and Madura purchased carnival games and concessions, and Indiana Gardens Amusement Park and Roller Rink opened on February 3, 1917.

Indiana Gardens featured dancing in the summer and roller-skating in the winter with the capacity to hold 1,000 people. General admission was 10¢, or 25¢ including skates for ladies and 35¢ with skates for gentlemen. Madura's ads emphasized the cleanliness and moral order of the place where the entire family was welcome, which was in contrast to the reputation of most dance halls of nearby Roby that were considered to be places of ill repute.

The founder of Madura's Danceland, Mike Madura, was a charismatic and energetic risk taker from the beginning. Pictured at left in 1908 at the age of 20, Madura was a member of the Northern Indiana Volunteer Firemen's Association. Below, Madura (far left) and his bride to be, Julia Cannon (second from left), celebrate the Fourth of July, 1911, in Milwaukee, Wisconsin. Milwaukee was near Julia's hometown of Port Washington, Wisconsin. The others in the photograph are unidentified. Mike (age 23) and Julia (age 19) were married on September 11, 1911, at Sacred Heart Church in Whiting, Indiana by Fr. Joseph Burke.

After earning a reputation as a successful manager at the Whiting Roller Rink, Madura partnered with Julius Linnemann to open the Indiana Gardens Roller Rink. Mike and Julia Madura's children, Evelyn (left, age 3) and Michael Jr. (right, age 5), are pictured on a winter day in 1918 at the amusement park. This is the only known existing picture of Indiana Gardens, which was open for five years from February 1917 to January 1922.

During World War I, Mike Madura's ads read, "Prepare for war now by building your body; make your muscles hard and your cheeks glow at Indiana Gardens." Races between the "World's Famous Pedestrian" Dan O'Leary (walking 1 mile) and skaters (skating 2.5 miles) occurred regularly, with prizes including a purse of $50 and a Dan O'Leary medal.

On February 1, 1919, Mike Madura bought out Linnemann's half of Indiana Gardens. Just 10 days later he bought a 3,000-pound white "Style 164 Military Band Organ" (as seen here) with motor and 30 music rolls from the Rudolph Wurlitzer Company in Chicago for $1,690. Some 28 of its 316 pipes were trumpets and 44 were brass "clarionettes" and piccolos. With the windows open, a person could hear the music from the imposing organ through the wilderness to North Hammond. These two financial notes made it difficult for Madura to run the business for profit for a while, but both the paucity of dance halls in Chicago (only White City, Midway Gardens, Merry Gardens, and Harmon's Dreamland) and the end of World War I were boons to business, and by 1920 Mike Madura was solidly on his feet. (Courtesy of Ron Bopp.)

Popular tunes of the World War I era were "K-K-K-Katy" (right), "the sensational stammering song success sung by the soldiers and sailors," written by Geoffrey O'Hara; "I'm Forever Blowing Bubbles" (below) by Jaan Kenbrovin and John W. Kellett; "Over There"; "I'm a Long Way from Tipperary"; and reflecting the dance craze, "I Wish I Could Shimmy Like My Sister Kate." Besides featuring organ music, Madura hired the four-piece bands (saxophone, violin, piano, and drums) of John Sterling and Cope Harvey for $40 a night. Mike's slogan for Indiana Gardens that lasted through the Danceland era was "Dance and Stay Young." (Both courtesy of the Indiana University Lilly Library.)

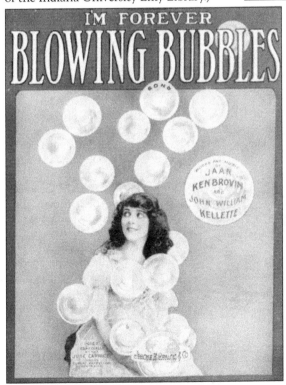

13

The beautiful Hammond Beach Inn opened during the summer of 1915. Thousands thronged to the elaborately decorated inn to dine and dance, fish, boat, or swim. After a dip in Lake Michigan waters (seen here), many of the beachgoers changed into their dress clothes and boarded a tram to Indiana Gardens Amusement Park.

This sketch by Michael (Mick) Madura Jr. is the only existing image of the Indiana Gardens park grounds. It shows the location, at the corner of Calumet Avenue and Indianapolis Boulevard, with streetcar lines, park entrance, café, roller rink, carousel, outdoor bar, picnic area, parking lot, Wolf Lake, and the frozen hydrant that failed to save Indiana Gardens from fire.

GENEVA HOUSE — FISH, CHICKEN, STEAK, AND FROG LEG DINNERS

1349 CALUMET AVE., AT INDIANAPOLIS BLVD., WHITING, IND.

Many restaurants at Five Points were destination spots as well, and they ranged from food shacks to sophisticated restaurants. The soul food of Whiting/Robertsdale was fresh local perch, as described by McKinlay in *Oil and Water: A Pictorial History of Whiting/ Robertsdale, Indiana.* Each restaurant prepared it in its own distinctive way, although boned and buttered was a favorite. Margaret's Geneva House (above) was located next door to where Danceland stood after 1929. Pete Levent's Barbecue (below), located at 1247 Calumet Avenue, and Vogel's Restaurant, originally located on Calumet Avenue but later moved to 1250 Indianapolis Boulevard, were also landmarks.

PHIL SMIDT & SON

Known the World Over

OPEN THE YEAR ROUND

Carl Lundgren's Restaurant (above) at 1205 Calumet Avenue later became the home of the famous Phil Smidt and Son Restaurant, which was originally located in Roby (left). A complete supper at Phil Smidt's restaurant of all-you-can-eat fresh perch, with potato salad, cottage cheese, coleslaw, pickled beets, kidney beans, potatoes, bread, butter, and coffee cost $1.25 as late as 1941, with a martini added for 25¢. This was the same favorite meal served until the restaurant closed in 2007. Phil Smidt's restaurant had a special aura not only because of its menu, but because guests could sit in one of the beautiful dining rooms or in the elegant bar with windows facing the railroad tracks and Lake Michigan.

Beginning in 1920, a meal served at Otto Roth's famous Blackhawk Restaurant and big band dance venue at Wabash Avenue and Randolph Street in the heart of Chicago's Loop featured similar fish dinners to those found at Phil Smidt's, Vogel's, and other fine restaurants at Five Points. For the cost of $1.50, a complete meal of fried soft shell crabs, broiled black sea bass, or fried filet of sole was available, while for $2 one could dine on the local favorites of fried frog legs, filet of pike, or broiled whitefish, complete with dessert. The Blackhawk featured dinner and dancing into the night.

M. MADURA
Manager Indiana Gardens Amusement Park

Has been skating for fifteen years, also operating a rink for eleven years at Whiting, Indiana, and made skating popular in Whiting, Hammond, East Chicago, Indiana Harbor, Gary and South Chicago. In 1918 he organized a basket ball team on roller skates. It proved very successful.

Despite the lively spirit of Five Points, Chicago-area winters were bleak. After the skaters had left on the cold night of January 31, 1922, Indiana Gardens Roller Rink was mysteriously consumed by fire. Mike Madura (left) sued the city of Hammond for negligence in providing adequate fire protection because the fire hydrants were frozen. Although Madura asked for $10,000 for property loss, Judge Maurice E. Crites of Mayor Daniel Brown's administration awarded him only $2,000 (below), suggesting careless use of stoves that heated the rink. Of that amount, $1,000 went to Mike Madura's attorney, William J. Whinery. The remaining $1,000 was just enough to pay off the land he had previously bought on the northeast side of Five Points, where he planned to build another rink. Six years later the land became the site of Madura's Danceland.

Wednesday, Feb. 7, 1923.

CITY RESPONSIBLE
FOR FIRE LOSS

Jury Gives Mike Madura $2,000 Damages For Loss of Rink.

Two

BOARDWALK PARK'S DANCELAND

Every major American city featured extravagant amusement parks, complete with carnival rides, arcades, and dance halls, and Chicago, the nation's second largest city, was no exception. Despite Prohibition, which began on January 16, 1920 (and lasted until December 5, 1933), the nation's prosperity was at an all-time high.

In 1925, a brand-new amusement park was being built across the street from the Madura home, which was located next to their landlord Lundgren's Restaurant at Five Points. The main entrance to the new park was on Indianapolis Boulevard near Roby in order to attract the Chicago crowd. Boardwalk Park was scheduled to open on May 22, 1926, with the world's largest roller coaster, the King Bee, on one end and a magnificent ballroom, Danceland, on the other. Admission to the park was free.

The $100,000 Danceland ballroom, with its highly publicized maple wood dance floor, had its grand opening on April 24, 1926—a full month before Boardwalk Park officially opened. The music of Walt "Happy" Hines and his Danceland orchestra was featured. Dancing was held every Tuesday, Thursday, and Friday night with a 20¢ admission charge. Candy nights, carnival nights, prize nights, and vaudeville stars were presented. A fashion show and beauty contest for the 50 most beautiful girls in northern Indiana was held June 1–5, 1926. Prizes to the top three finalists included a diamond ring, a wristwatch, a pearl necklace, and three engraved silver cups, all totaling $500 in cash value. Mayors Adrian E. Tinkham of Hammond and Floyd E. Williams of Gary presented the awards.

Other features were demonstrations and lessons in the Charleston offered by Buddy and Arline Anderson, dance contest winners at Chicago's Trianon Ballroom, as well as fox trot, waltz, and Charleston dance contests. Hit songs of that 1925–1926 season were "Yes Sir, That's My Baby," "Show Me the Way to Go Home," "Always," "Five Foot Two," and "Sometimes I'm Happy."

PASS TO
DANCELAND
BOARDWALK PARK
INDIANAPOLIS BOULEVARD AND 112TH STREET
(NEAR ROBY)
HAMMOND, INDIANA

Mr.——————————————————*and Lady*

Issued by——————————————

NOT GOOD SATURDAYS, SUNDAYS OR HOLIDAYS   375

In the summer of 1926, six dance bands were advertised to play continuous music from 8:30 p.m. until the morning. The bands were Happy Hines; Gene Goldkette's Victor Recording Orchestra, featuring Bix Beiderbecke and Frank Trumbauer; the Midway Gardens Orchestra; Jinks Bryan and his Chicago Yacht Club Orchestra; Charlie Pierce and his Illianians; and the Six Chicago Jazz Kings.

After the Indiana Gardens fire, Mike Madura became an ironworker and the first president of the International Association of Bridge, Structural, and Ornamental Iron Workers, Local 395. In this photograph on the job, Madura is in the front row to the far left. With energy to spare after 10 hours a day of hard labor, he would head to Boardwalk Park to be a professional barker.

The three children of Mike and Julia Madura posed for this 1925 photograph (above) at Boardwalk Park. From left to right are Michael Jr. (13), Evelyn (11), and Doris (4). Michael Jr. (Mick) worked with his father at their Boardwalk Park Ball 'Em Out concession, for which he was paid between $1 and $2 a day. Mike's record for the week (below) of July 10, 1928, also indicates a profit of $70 for that week. The concession grossed over $4,900 during one summer season, which was enough for the Maduras to buy a house on Roberts Avenue in Whiting.

BALL 'EM OUT

Ball Game

FOR

Parks and Carnivals

Patented by J. D. PONTIOUS

708 Price Place
HAMMOND, INDIANA

Manufactured by
PONTIOUS & MADURA
708 Price Place
HAMMOND, INDIANA

PATENTED MAY 23rd 1927 ~ BY J. D. PONTIOUS ~ HAMMOND, IND.

OUR SLIDE BALL GAME

Mike Madura partnered with J. D. Pontious, who invented the Ball 'Em Out carnival game. This concession consisted of a series of doors set back about 16 feet, and each player, who would get three sponge rubber balls for a dime, would try to hit the knobs on each door. If a direct hit was made, a lady in a bathing suit would slide out and hand the customer a box of chocolates. Michael Jr. was the chief ball boy and occasional rookie barker, even while his adolescent voice change was occurring. He commented years later, "Every kid should get such a job. Calling to the midway crowd to play your game over and over not only strengthens the vocal muscles and lessens timidity, but teaches a boy how to work under pressure, including making change correctly and quickly."

The Madura's Ball 'Em Out concession on the Boardwalk midway was directly below the second dip of the King Bee roller coaster. The screams of the riders and squeals of the wheels could be heard for blocks around Five Points. The four-car coaster jerked and shot up and down for more than a half mile along Calumet Avenue, over the Danceland ballroom, and toward its Indianapolis Boulevard starting point, where it was manually braked to a thumping halt. Other features of the park included the Storm-At-Sea, the Chute-the-Chutes, the Whip, a $10,000 carousel, a 60-foot-tall Ferris wheel, a shooting gallery, Skee-Ball alleys, and an airplane swing that gave riders a breathtaking view of Lake Michigan.

In 1927, Danceland experienced upgrades costing $10,000, which included upholstered seating that encircled the entire ballroom floor. Another improvement was new lighting in the huge arch that spanned the floor and in the two giant chandeliers (measuring 21 feet in diameter) to create changing color effects. More than 200 different circuits and switches were necessary to manipulate the lighting. In each chandelier there were 36 blue bulbs, 36 reds, 36 greens, and four large whites. The spectacular lighting combined with its "spring-cushioned" dance floor made Danceland an extremely desirable place for a romantic evening of dancing. The famous floor made of maple wood absorbed shock, making it easy on the feet and legs of dancers. It was designed to "breathe" with natural air pressure, even under a weight of 900,000 pounds—the approximate weight of 6,000 people, which was the ballroom's capacity.

In 1928, the concession tenants wondered about the rumors that Boardwalk Park, only three years old, would be razed because Lever Brothers soap company wanted to buy the land. Although crowds on weekends were good, the park couldn't compete with the White City Amusement Park or the fabulous Trianon Ballroom (seen here) at Sixty-Second Street and Cottage Grove Avenue in Chicago.

One thing that saved Danceland from demolition was the leasing of the ballroom to W. G. Newbould, a marathon dance promoter, who is said to have cleared $85,000 for the venture. Although Boardwalk Park closed permanently after the 1928 summer season, Danceland drew customers heavily into the cold months as couples competed for the $5,000 prize in the dance marathon contest.

The rules for governing the World's Championship Marathon Endurance Dance mandated that all men be clean and clean-shaven and that all contestants wear white hosiery and remain in dancing position with feet moving and one hand on their partners at all times. They were not allowed within 3 feet of other dancers or the guide rope. Arguing, smoking, speaking with spectators, or leaving the dance floor for air without their trainer was forbidden. One bell signal during dancing indicated the beginning of a rest period, and one bell signal during resting indicated that it was time to resume dancing. Two bells signaled a three-minute warning during the rest period, because if the starting bell sounded and the contestants were not in proper dance position, they were eliminated from the contest.

NORA RYAN
CHICAGO'S VENUS
WORLD'S CHAMPIONSHIP MARATHON ENDURANCE DANCE
HAMMOND, IND.   W.G. NEWBOULD, PROMOTER
BOARDWALK PARK
CALUMET STUDIO
CHICAGO

Marathon contestants came to Boardwalk Park's Danceland from Whiting, Hammond, East Chicago, Indiana Harbor, LaPorte and South Bend, Indiana; Chicago and Calumet City, Illinois; Milwaukee, Wisconsin; Houston, Texas; New York City; and Pennsylvania. Spectators sat all day and all night cheering their favorite dance teams on. One group included Al Capone, who sat down in the lower bleacher seats about two nights a week, probably appreciating the Indiana hideaway. Live music was provided by the Urbanek orchestra Rags and His Ginger Snaps from Chicago. A highlight of the championship marathon was a wedding between contestant Bobby Dixon of East Chicago and Odie Quinn, a local Whiting non-contestant on September 27, 1928. This photograph shows the winners of the World's Championship Marathon Endurance Dance, Nora Ryan and her partner. The famous maple wood dance floor and band stage can be seen.

Despite Danceland's success, the dismantling of Boardwalk Park was scheduled for the spring of 1929. Lever Brothers of Cambridge, Massachusetts, was buying the land for a reported $250,000 to make room for a new Lux soap plant. Mike Madura was eyeing the idle ballroom and began having visions of moving the huge structure to his land. A contractor told him that he could move it "but with some reservations."

```
        -:     M O R T G A G E      :-

Mike Madura and
Julia Madura, his wife,

     To

Bank of Whiting, Whiting,
Indiana, as Trustee.

     Mortgage for $12,821.19, dated July 19th, 1929, acknowledged
regularly on July 20th, 1929, by Mike Madura and Julia Madura, his
wife, before Catherine Mackin, Notary Public, Lake County, Indiana,
and recorded July 22nd, 1929, in Mortgage Record  365  page  197

     MORTGAGE AND WARRANT:  Lots number twenty-five (25), twenty-
six (26) and twenty-seven (27), in Block number One (1) of Forsyth's
Sheffield Subdivision, in the City of Hammond, Lake County, Indiana,
with all rights, privileges, and appurtenances thereto belonging.
```

When his father brought the news home that he had bought the ballroom, Mick, who was 16 at the time recalled, "It was like a dream come true." Daughter Evelyn remembered, "He mortgaged the house, the land, everything except the suit on his back!" The second mortgage (seen here) likely covered the purchase of the ballroom, the move, and renovations.

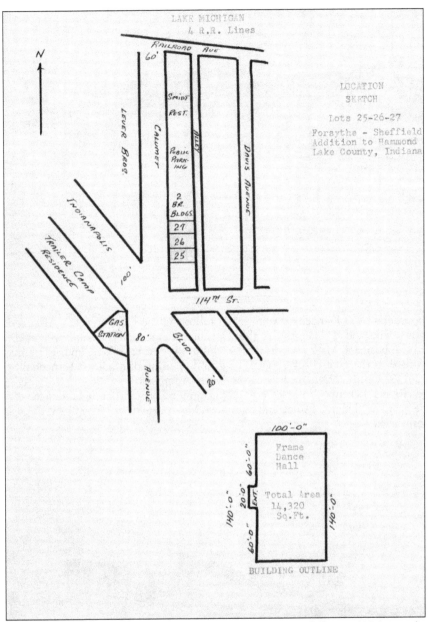

LAKE MICHIGAN
4 R.R. Lines

RAILROAD AVE
60'

N

LEVER BROS.

CALUMET

INDIANAPOLIS

TRAILER CAMP
RESIDENCE

SMIDT
REST.

PUBLIC
PARK-
ING

2
BR.
BLDGS.

27
26
25

ALLEY

DAVIS AVENUE

LOCATION
SKETCH

Lots 25-26-27

Forsythe - Sheffield
Addition to Hammond
Lake County, Indiana

100'

GAS
STATION   80'

AVENUE

BLVD.

80'

114TH ST.

100'-0"

140'-0"   20'-0"   60'-0"

ENT.

60'-0"

Frame
Dance
Hall

Total Area
14,320
Sq.Ft.

140'-0"

BUILDING OUTLINE

On May 11, 1929, the 42-year-old Mike Madura contracted John Ahlborn of Hammond to move the 14,320-square-foot building from the park to his land a quarter mile away at 1337 Calumet Avenue. The cost of the move was $6,000—almost twice the cost to buy it. It was moved in one section, a job that took over three months. A horse team pulled the giant structure inch by inch on a windlass, which attracted people from miles around. Calumet Avenue was blocked for days, upsetting beachgoers and proprietors of local businesses, while telephone poles and trees were removed and sidewalks were cracked. A windstorm caused the ballroom to weave back and forth; all of the lights and toilets broke. Finally Danceland was firmly maneuvered between two buildings and lowered to the ground after both ends were cut off and the entire frontage removed so the mammoth room would fit on the 150-foot lot Mike Madura had the foresight to buy years before.

These photographs of Danceland were taken following the move in 1929. After repairs and renovations, Mike added "Madura's" to the "Danceland" sign, and the family affair began. Mike managed the business, Mick and his mother, Julia, were ticket takers, and sisters Evelyn and Doris worked in the coat-check room. The grand opening of Madura's Danceland came on August 24, 1929, with 2,974 dancers in attendance. Admission was 50¢ and roses were given to the ladies. Russell Eckenboy's 10-piece band of Hammond played that night for a fee of $90. The first tune heard at Madura's Danceland was "Love Me or Leave Me." The Great Depression was just months away.

Three

MADURA'S DANCELAND AND THE GREAT DEPRESSION

When Madura's Danceland first opened for business in August 1929, the onset of the Great Depression had not yet occurred. Even the stock market crash on Black Thursday (October 24, 1929) was not felt immediately due to the robustness of the Chicago area's dance scene. Madura's Danceland was open six nights a week for an admission charge of 50¢ for ladies and 75¢ for gentlemen and paid the bands between $150 and $300 per night. In 1930, it upgraded its sound system from a megaphone, which had been used for announcements and singing, to its first microphone and sound system (a five-tube, six-watt amplifier with five speakers).

However, by the end of 1930 many of the nation's ballrooms began to close, as dancers could no longer afford the cost of travel and admission. The stock market then embarked on a steady decline from April 1931 to July 1932 to the lowest it had been since the 19th century. By the end of 1933, half of the nation's banks had closed (in fact, Hammond was the largest city in the nation in which every bank closed). As a result, band pay at Danceland was reduced from triple to double figures, and many agreed to play for 50 percent of the ticket sales for the evening. This policy resulted in some local bands being paid as little as $5 a night. Fortunately traveling musicians' living costs were low. One night's lodging plus three meals cost only $2, and most musicians felt that working for a little money was better than not working at all.

The fact that bands continued to work and that Danceland stayed open for business is remarkable in light of the nation's financial devastation. As bleak as the economy was, people still wanted to dance in order to forget their cares, and Madura's Danceland offered them an escape from the hard times. Lowered admission prices, admission-free Tuesdays for ladies who came in before 8:00 p.m., and Sunday matinee dances were successful business strategies. Many young men would walk all the way from the East Side of Chicago or pile as many as possible into a car to get to Danceland.

NEWS FLASHES
MADURA'S DANCELAND
Five Points, Hammond, Indiana

Vol. 1   Published Weekly in the Interest of Good Dancing   Sat., Nov. 16th, 1929

GALA FASHION SHOW REVIEW!
Saturday and Sunday, November 23 and 24

New Orchestra Opens at Danceland in a Blaze of Dance Glory

The Utmost in Dance Music! Art Miller and His Famous Recording Orchestra!

The management of Madura's Danceland feel that they have made

ART MILLER

a move that will please the most exacting of ball-room dancers by bringing Art Miller and his famous recording orchestra to Hammond for the balance of the entire winter season.

This great orchestra has attained a position in the musical world second to none. They offer that irresistible style of dance music that through their phonograph recordings have made them known nationally.

Dance lovers have the pleasure of enjoying this music every Tuesday, Thursday, Saturday and Sunday nights.

(Continued on page 3)

Eighteen Beautiful Girl Models

Staged and Coached by E. Leinen Dance Master

Gorgeous Evening Gowns, Snappy Sport Costumes, Chic Street Dresses, and Beautiful Winter Coats, Displayed on a dazzling illuminated runway on the dance floor, by eighteen beautiful girl models selected from the dancers and coached by E. Leinen Dance Master.

All of the Coats, Dresses, and Frocks, displayed at this stupendous production are furnished through the courtesy and cooperation of BROWNS DRESS SHOPPE located at 2961 East 92nd St., South Chicago's leading.

(Continued on page 2)

Not Too Personal

Eva Borman, Say Eva, how does it feel to get up and broadcast with all these good looking musicians. And by the way, who's the new boy friend who keeps waving the nice little piece of paper at you?

We're betting that Anna Kovach will be looking around for another dance marathon, now that she and the boy friend are on the outs.

Say, finding what is Nick coming back to try out our dance floor? Why not invite him out? We know that after the first dance, everything will be O. K.

(Continued on page 2)

Behind the Scenes With Art Miller and Red Leinen

Forecast of Coming Events

Red—"Well, Art, you've been playing here for a week now, what do you think of Danceland and all us girls and boys?"

Art—"Why, I'll tell you, Red—I've been playing all over the middle west for the past six years and I don't believe I've ever met, or had the pleasure of playing for such a wonderful crowd as dancers. I'm certainly glad that I'm going to be here for the rest of the winter season. I know that when we are more accustomed we are going to have some pleasant times. I have a lot of novel ideas in my bag of tricks and I'm sure that they will meet with the approval of the most discriminating. But, just because I have all those ideas, doesn't mean that I am accomplishing them alone, as I am appreciating just as my associates in helping to furnish the best in entertainment features that you possibly can had. With your cooperation we will be able to have something new every night. I'll furnish the inspiration for the rest."

Red—"What Art, I was thinking—"

Art—"I, is it possible?"

Red—"All kidding aside, every Tuesday night I have chosen our class night and I have fifty girls and boys who are assisting me in instructing and we guarantee to teach anyone how to dance in one night."

Art—"Say, that's wonderful, Red, but how about Thursday nights?"

Red—"Well, this coming Tuesday we're going to have a pillow fight and a week from Thursday we're going to have the big Thanksgiving.

(Continued on page 2)

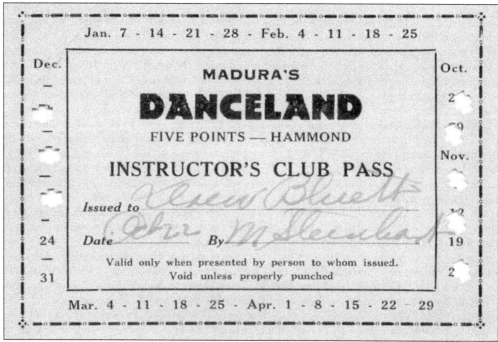

The Instructor's Dance Club, pictured on the cover of this book, held lessons at Madura's Danceland every Tuesday evening in 1929. The holder of the Instructor's Club pass pictured here attended the dance on October 22, just two days before the stock market crashed. The pass holder returned the next week on Black Tuesday, when stocks dropped lower than any previous time in history, and continued coming for several weeks.

This 1929 newsletter written by Mick Madura announces the upcoming appearance of the Art Miller Recording Orchestra at Danceland. The known musicians in the band were Art Miller, director; Lee Armentrout, trombone; Verne Lindo, trumpet; Floyd Rogers, piano; and Johnny Craig, drums.

FIRST ANNUAL DANCE

Given By

DANCELAND CLUB

At

DANCELAND

1214

Ladies 50c   **Feb. 26, 1930**

Despite the stock market crash, Madura's Danceland recorded a crowd of 6,200, its second largest of all time, on November 13, 1929, for the Hammond Fraternal Order of Police dance. Other large events were the balls of the International Alliance of Theatrical Stage Employees and Motion Picture Machine Operators and the Danceland Dance Club, both in February 1930.

The Democratic Central Committee sponsored the Lake County Celebration and Dance at Danceland on June 24, 1931. Officers were John A. Tokarz and Whiting mayor Thomas S. Boyle (pictured). That same year, the Lake County Voters' League, led by George Clements, held a nonpartisan assembly of 2,000 people. It opened with a speech by Secretary of State Otto Fifield and ended with a grand march led by Walter Green, Hammond city clerk.

IN PERSON

ONE NIGHT ONLY   ONE NIGHT ONLY

One of the three Hottest Dance Or-chestra's in the World

ERSKINE TATE

"The Sultan of Jazz'
and his great

Colored Orchestra

Hear Chicago's highest paid colored dance orchestra in Indiana's largest Ballroom

SAT., NOV. 7th

MADURA'S

DANCELAND

Five Points — Hammond, Ind.
Ladies 50c   Gentlemen 75c
Dancing 8:30 p. m. to 2:00 a. m.

Madura's Danceland, located 15 miles south of downtown Chicago, took advantage of that city's vibrant early dance band scene. One outstanding bandleader was jazz violinist Erskine Tate (left), who played on November 7, 1931. Tate's orchestra likely included Louis Armstrong and others from the Vendome Theater, where they had played for a decade. Other great early bands were led by trumpeters Joe "King" Oliver in May 1931, Bernie Young in December 1930, "Wild Bill" Davison in November 1931, Louis Panico in July 1932, and pianist Charley Straight (below) in May 1933. This hot dance music had its origins in New Orleans style but had the driving energy of Chicago.

Knights of Holy Trinity

PRESENT

Charley Straight

AND HIS

C - B - S Orchestra

FEATURING

Peggy Clawson

"Radio's Personality Girl"

Wed., May 17, 1933

AT

DANCELAND

FIVE POINTS   HAMMOND

Entree at 8 P. M.

ADMISSION - 35c per person

One of the best big bands of the late 1920s and early 1930s was the Detroit-based McKinney's Cotton Pickers (right), who competed successfully with Duke Ellington and Fletcher Henderson (and in fact hired Henderson's arranger, Don Redman). An important recording was "Gee Baby Ain't I Good to You," with renowned band members Fats Waller, Coleman Hawkins, Benny Carter, Doc Cheatham, and Rex Stewart. Their theme song was "If I Could Be With You" (below). They appeared at Danceland on August 29, 1931, and with an admission charge of 75¢ for ladies and $1.25 for gentlemen, the Maduras enjoyed an ample profit of $225 that Depression-era evening.

"Indiana's Largest and Most Beautiful Ballroom"

CIRCULATION OVER 5,500

MADURA'S DANCELAND NEWSETTE

DANCING TUESDAY THURSDAY SATURDAY SUNDAY & HOLIDAYS

Calumet Ave. and Indianapolis Blvd.

Five Points, Hammond, Indiana

VOL. I.   THURSDAY, AUGUST 24, 1933.   PUBLISHED MONTHLY

BOB-KAYES BAND OPENS HUGE LABOR DAY PROGRAM

SUE PRIDALA CHRISTENS DANCELAND'S "NEWSETTE"

This is the initial completion of the new and herald Danceland Newsette compiled and edited by Mickey Madura who is making painstaking effort in developing the Danceland Newsette into a colorful and interesting ballroom newspaper. The first problem to confront the editors and arrangers was to seek a title; one that had distinction and discrimination, yet full in color and one that was different from those of other ballrooms. A title contest was immediately laid out; columns written in various newspapers; announcements sent out and many other types of advertising displayed. A fortnight had hardly passed when over four hundred and sixty-eight responses were received and the half dozen judges were set to work. At the termination of the contest and the entire list of names carefully selected and examined only one name or title seemed to reach the expectations of the judges. It was "Newsette" and none other than Miss Sue Pridala who resides at 3805 Fir Street in good ol' East Chicago, Indiana, was the young lady that sent in the famous title. This title is truly famous as it may live forever as a trade-mark, but there is a possible chance that the name may be changed probably after the third issue or more. The contest judges for the new enterprise were Herbert J. Robinson of the Evening American; Mr. F. Horne of the Herald and Examiner; Jack Thompson and Phil Novak of the Lake County Times; Roy A. Barton of the New York Herald; Joe Progar and yours truly of the ballroom. Honorable mentions may be published providing the title senders agree to the idea; that is, in the following issue. Incidently, Miss Pridala is subject to two season tickets which were offered in an advertisement a short time ago. Her title was chosen mostly for its clearness and vividness, notwithstanding the fact that there is much significance connected as to different classes of people that shall receive the Newsette. Congratulations, Sue. To the victor belongs the spoils.

D'ARMOUR LAUDS DANCERS OF DANCELAND

Jack D'Armour may never be forgotten as far as the Danceland goers are concerned. No, it wasn't exactly his music, but because of the statement he made before he departed Sunday night after closing hours August 6. You are probably amazed to wonderment as to what sort of criticizing would arouse ones curiosity of a dance orchestra director! Well, here are his vivid words: "Never have I come in contact with such particular dancers before in my days as a musical director. I have been directing

many orchestras throughout the country during the last twelve years and I don't hesitate to state that the Madura's Danceland patrons are very hard to please. Of course that made the job more interesting, but still I am inclined to think the dancers are just a bit too exact. (Editor's note—Maybe he meant too fussy?) They don't seem to overlook a thing. Especially after a six-week engagement I really ought to visualize them more clearly, but sorrowfully I must admit the impossible. I only hope to return once again and do my utmost."

Continued on page 3

BOB KAYE'S ORCHESTRA TO OPEN THE GALA LABOR DAY PARTY

Cancel all engagements! Make it a point to attend Madura's Danceland Labor Day, Monday, September 4! Why? Because Mike Madura has signed the musical sensation of the year, and it's none other than Bobby Kaye and his famous orchestra from the far west. Yes, sir; they hail from the state of Montana, where men are strong and healthy and the women have to like it.

Now that the editor feels he has the reader enthused and interested, he'll continue with a bit of formality and sincerity. Bob Kaye and his orchestra begins an indefinite engagement (possibly a month), and let's all give him a happy and joyous "first night." He has twelve supermusicians in his invincible lance orchestra who are graduates of the Montana University. This well-known aggregation has been organized seven years and are stepping at a fast clip to the top. Bobby has entertained the stay-uplaters at the Milwaukee Roof, Long Beach Pier in Los Angeles and has thrilled the dancers at the Arcadia room in New York. He has found business at a low ebb at many of these places, but within a short time the increase was so tremendous the managers demanded renewal of contract. Bob has refused these new contracts as he wishes to travel and is of the progressing type. Critics say he is foolish to do this, but Bob thinks differently, a ohere is a chance to dance and enjoy the melodious dance music ever to be presented to the public. The admission for this gala occasion is 25 cents for the ladies and 25 cents for the gentlemen. Photographs of the entire band are to be seen in main entrance. The ladies might take special notice to the photos as the men are quite handsome. It might be well to add that the orchestral setup is one of the flashiest ever. The music stands

Continued on page 2

HAL KEMP HERE SEPT. 26TH

Hal Kemp and his international favorites who have been doing a tremendous business for Otto Roth's Blackhawk Cafe plays a one nigh stand at Madrid Danceland ball room. They have been scheduled by the Knights of Holy Trinity of Indiana Harbor.

One of the largest crowds of the year is expected to dance to the music of the Kemp style. They are being booked through the M. C. A. of Chicago. Kemp leaves for a four month tour so here's your last opportunity to hear him.

Mick Madura created all of the Danceland advertisements, including the monthly *Newsette*. It had a circulation of 5,500 and was developed based on the Music Corporation of America's *Advertising Guide for Dance Managers* as well as samples from the Trianon and Aragon Ballrooms in Chicago. It provided patrons with announcements of upcoming dances, historical facts and quizzes about the bands, photographs, and local gossip and jokes. The August 24, 1930, issue announces the appearance of Hal Kemp, his co-arrangers John Scott Trotter (pianist) and Wendell Mayhew (trombonist), and his drummer "Skinnay" Ennis, who sang the theme song "Got a Date with an Angel." A large crowd was expected, but the audience numbered only 40. Admission was 50¢ for ladies and 75¢ for gentlemen in advance, and 60¢ or 90¢, respectively, at the door. Kemp agreed to play for 50 percent of the ticket sales that night, paying his band only $20.

"Tweet" Hogan played at Madura's Danceland in 1929, 1933, and 1934. A local Chicagoan and graduate of Loyola University, he organized an orchestra that played widely on campuses and then gained much notoriety through performances at the finest hotels in Chicago and on the air via WGN, NBC, and WCCO.

Bandleader and drummer Bernie Cummins appeared at Madura's Danceland in November 1933. Originally from Ohio, his band enjoyed much success at New York's Biltmore, Roosevelt, and New Yorker Hotels and later at Chicago's Trianon and Aragon Ballrooms, which broadcast over WGN. Widely recorded on Gennett, Brunswick, and Victor, the band played a variety of styles from hot jazz to novelty pieces. "Minnie the Mermaid" was a big Victor hit.

MUSIC CORPORATION OF AMERICA
NEW YORK - CHICAGO

Presents

MAURIE SHERMAN

AND HIS

ORCHESTRA

SATURDAY, OCTOBER 17th

DANCELAND

Five Points — Hammond, Ind.

CHICAGO'S FAVORITE SOCIETY ORCHESTRA
DIRECT FROM COLLEGE INN

Other name band leaders who appeared during the Depression era were Maurie Sherman (former violinist with Isham Jones), Charlie Agnew (who led one of the best "sweet" bands for dancing), Frankie Masters (a fine guitarist, singer, and bandleader), Clyde McCoy (famous for his "wah-wah" trumpet style), Ace Brigode, Jack Chapman, George Devron, Carson Donnelly, Art Kassel, Bob Kaye, Dell Lampe, Correy Lynn, Carl "Deacon" Moore, Eddie Neibauer, Don Pedro, Jack Russell, and Junie Cobb. The following bands that played at Madura's Danceland between 1929 and 1933 are assumed to be regional bands: Dorothy Aldrich, Shan Austin, Frank Cibular, Jack D'Armour, Jack Doll, Chuck Garber, Joe Gerken, Dell Hamelen, Bob Jackson, Half Pint Jackson, Glenn Johnson, Dave Kahue, Jay Kenny, Burt Kestrin, Don Kirkham, Billy Michaels, Joe Nitte, Frankie Oller, Matt Rhem, George Sherry, Dick Smith, Tommy Thompson, and Bus Widmer.

Junie Cobb and his Grains of Corn appeared at Danceland on November 21, 1931, directly from Paris, France. Cobb was born in Arkansas, attended the University of New Orleans, and migrated to Chicago, where he worked as a banjo player with Earl Hines and King Oliver. A versatile musician, his recordings feature him as a composer, pianist, clarinetist, saxophonist, vocalist, and violinist. (Courtesy of Stephen G. McShane.)

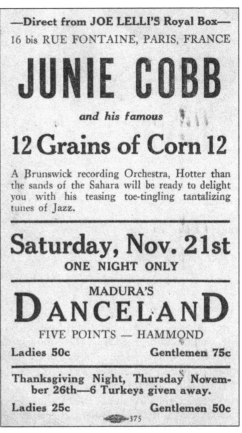

—Direct from JOE LELLI'S Royal Box—
16 bis RUE FONTAINE, PARIS, FRANCE

JUNIE COBB

and his famous

12 Grains of Corn 12

A Brunswick recording Orchestra, Hotter than the sands of the Sahara will be ready to delight you with his teasing toe-tingling tantalizing tunes of Jazz.

Saturday, Nov. 21st
ONE NIGHT ONLY

MADURA'S
DANCELAND
FIVE POINTS — HAMMOND

Ladies 50c   Gentlemen 75c

Thanksgiving Night, Thursday November 26th—6 Turkeys given away.

Ladies 25c   Gentlemen 50c
375

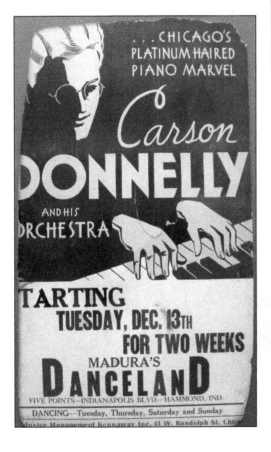

...CHICAGO'S PLATINUM HAIRED PIANO MARVEL
Carson DONNELLY
AND HIS ORCHESTRA
STARTING TUESDAY, DEC. 13TH FOR TWO WEEKS
MADURA'S DANCELAND
FIVE POINTS—INDIANAPOLIS BLVD.—HAMMOND, IND.
DANCING—Tuesday, Thursday, Saturday and Sunday
Exclusive Management Kennaway Inc. 64 W. Randolph St. Chicago

Carson Donnelly, called the "Platinum-Haired Piano Marvel," enjoyed a two-week stay at Madura's Danceland in December 1932. Originally from Chicago, he gained recognition as co-leader of the Noble and Donnelly Goldcoasters Orchestra of the Drake Hotel. He later led his own band and performed in leading hotels around the Midwest.

The Chicago-area weather and its well-known lake-effect blizzards, floods, and heat waves kept the Maduras concerned with the comfort and safety of their clientele. By night, they appeared calm and cool in their three-piece suits, starched white shirts, and ties, but by day they were heavy manual laborers who shoveled snow off the dome roof to prevent it from caving in. They hauled and shoveled coal into the two furnaces to keep the mammoth space warm in the winter, and they created the illusion of cool weather on hot summer evenings with blue lighting and multiple fans. Above, a 1931 flood encroaches upon Danceland's door, and below, the dome roof is made invisible by a complete blanket of snow.

Four

YOU CAN'T SHIMMY AT MADURA'S DANCELAND

Chicago was as important a dance band scene as New York during the 1920s and 1930s. Chicago's unique combination of a dancing public, excellent bands, numerous performance venues, strong musicians' unions, competitive band booking agencies, and a dynamic radio broadcast industry made it "the cradle of the dance band business," according to Charles Sengstock in *That Toddlin' Town*. Social dancing had become more refined, and the era of the great public ballrooms had arrived. Ballrooms were generally much larger and more elegant than dance halls, a term that had negative connotations associated with alcohol and prostitution. Because Chicago had no laws to regulate dance halls, the Juvenile Protective Association (JPA) became the unofficial overseer of ballroom etiquette. It conducted investigations into the use of alcohol, dress codes, supervision, and conduct and worked with ballroom owners to enforce rules. The JPA objected to dance tempos that encouraged suggestive body movements, and despite enormous popularity, the shimmy was especially prohibited, as it was not a dance with steps, but rather a fast shaking of the upper body. As a result, the foxtrot became the preferred ballroom dance, not only because it was accessible to amateurs and allowed some creative freedom, but because it conformed to more traditional values. Madura's Danceland held to the same moral standards of the JPA.

Two important events in 1933 that boosted the dance band business near the end of the Depression years were the repeal of the 13-year-long Prohibition era, and the Century of Progress World's Fair situated along Chicago's Lake Michigan shoreline. Danceland's proximity to that city provided a unique opportunity for a variety of excellent bands to visit northwest Indiana's dancing public. In addition, the advent of radio broadcasting from ballrooms was the most important boon of the entire big band era. As the Depression was coming to a close, Madura's Danceland was going strong, yielding close to $9,000 yearly.

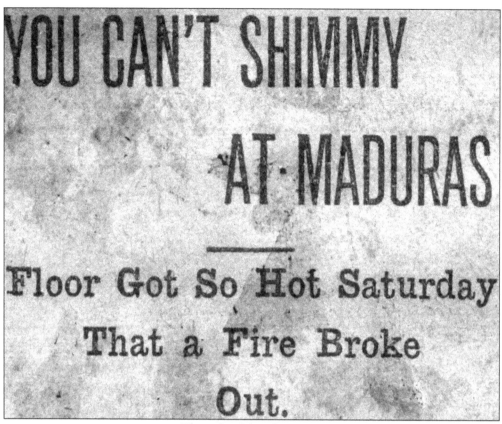

YOU CAN'T SHIMMY AT·MADURAS

Floor Got So Hot Saturday That a Fire Broke Out.

The title of this chapter came from a clever newspaper headline after a small fire broke out but was quickly extinguished. Mike Madura had little patience with patrons who broke the house rules. If he observed lewd dancing (which was inevitable if "Tiger Rag" was played), he would physically throw the offending man out.

Dancing Attire for Men is Enforced

Now that Summer has faded away and with it departed the terrifing heat, new rules and regulations are in vogue. The men will find this column rather interesting since it is written entirely for them. These rules are not in any way difficult to understand or obey. No. 1, Refrain from taking off suit coat at all times. Any man who wishes to make a good appearance before the ladies will never dance with his coat off. Only a very small percentage of the Danceland gentlemen are careless about these things, but let's make it a hundred per cent in adequate attire. The management doesn't enjoy the idea of reminding anyone during the dance session. No. 2. Sweatshirts and sweaters are strickly forbidden, unless worn beneath a suit coat; naturally a shirt must be an attache. No. 3. A man who attends a dance with a neatly tied tie is always at ease especially while dancing. The three rules are strictly enforced and anyone who continues to disobey them must expect rejection.

The dress code was described by 21-year-old Mick Madura in this October 1933 *Newsette*. The three rules stated, "Refrain from taking off suit coat at all times. . . . Sweatshirts and sweaters are strictly forbidden. . . . A man who attends a dance with a neatly tied tie is always at ease." Ties were loaned at the ticket box by Julia Madura if needed.

For ladies, satin was the 1933 fabric of choice for ballroom dancing. The *Newsette* carried ads for Dayton's store on State and Hohman Streets in Hammond. Dayton's sold "dance frocks in all the newest colors: black, brown, tile" for $7.95 and "Sunday night dresses . . . just right for any dance" for $3.95.

The Hall of Science was exhibited at the Century of Progress World's Fair of 1933 and 1934. The fair was located on 424 acres of Lake Michigan shoreline between Twelfth and Thirty-ninth Streets and was within walking distance of Chicago's downtown. The massive influx of people to the city created a need for more entertainment, which was a windfall for the dance band business.

WF-5   HALL OF SCIENCE, CHICAGO WORLD'S FAIR

3A-H340

The theme of the Century of Progress International Exposition was technological innovation, of which the automobile craze was a focus. The photograph above overlooks the General Motors Pavilion, which exhibited a working vehicle assembly line where fairgoers could watch their own Chevrolet being built. A souvenir of a first date between Mick Madura and his future wife was this jewelry box, seen below, topped with an aerial view of the fair looking south over Lake Michigan to Whiting, Indiana, just a few miles down Lake Shore Drive. The jewelry box is labeled "A Century of Progress: International Exposition Chicago 1933."

Radio played a critical role in the rise in popularity of the big bands after the Depression years. In 1934, dance music was reported to be the most popular form of radio entertainment, and on August 21, 1935, a broadcast of the Benny Goodman Orchestra from the Palomar Ballroom in Los Angeles (right) jump-started the swing era. Thinking ahead, Mike Madura had contracted for the installation of radio station WIND in Gary for $400 per month, and Danceland began its live broadcasts on New Year's Eve 1933, which continued for three years, and then resumed in 1938. The final broadcasting arrangement with WIND ran from 1939 until 1942. Mick Madura (below to the far right near the WIND microphone) was the announcer for eight live broadcasts four nights a week for all seven years.

THE

Palomar

THE DINING, DANCING AND ENTERTAINMENT CENTER OF THE WEST

presents

In 1934, Mick Madura's girlfriend listened to his radio broadcasts and transcribed her future husband's every word for three months. On November 20, 1934, she wrote, "Ladies and Gentlemen: Dancers prefer Madura's Danceland because of its smooth spring-cushioned dance floor and because Joe Chromis is in the musical spotlight. The place is Madura's Danceland at Indianapolis Boulevard where we will remain till 12 o'clock. The dance begins with Joe Chromis who directs his band from the piano on 'Have a Little Dream on Me'. . . . It's danceable, it's swingable, it's singable, it's 'Sweetie Pie' featuring Bob Harmison on vocals. . . . Now we hear Joe Chromis play those three famous words, 'I'm in Love'. . . . We dance again and it's 'Stay as Sweet as You Are' for Henrietta Kaminski of Hammond, Indiana." This was followed by a note in the margin that read, "Who could help being sweet to you, Sweetheart? I love you." She continued, "And the curtain comes down on tonight's broadcast. You have been listening from Madura's Danceland. Your station is WIND, the tip-top spot on your dial. Your announcer? Mick Madura. Good evening."

The May 1934 playlist (right) of the Joe Chromis Band was used by Mick Madura for his radio broadcast. Bob Harmison (below), the vocalist of the band, is seen in a 1934 photograph. His featured songs included "True," "She Reminds Me of You," "Riptide," "You Oughta Be in Pictures," and "Cocktails for Two." Other bandleaders who enjoyed success at Danceland during the late Depression years of 1934 to 1936 were Gene Cook, Bill Curran, Hal Denham, Lew Diamond, Byron Dunbar, Charles Gaylord, Earl Gray, "Skinnay" Hamp, Paul Hau, Elmer Kaiser, Jack Kirkpatrick, Carlos Molina, Marv Mytar, Primo Perozzi, Leo Remillard, and Nick Wonderlick.

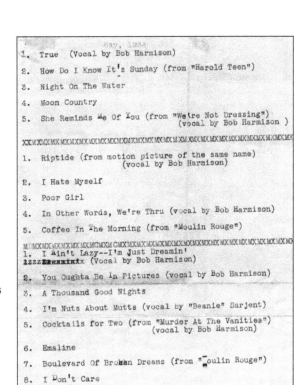

May, 1934

1. True (Vocal by Bob Harmison)

2. How Do I Know It's Sunday (from "Harold Teen")

3. Night On The Water

4. Moon Country

5. She Reminds Me Of You (from "We're Not Dressing") (vocal by Bob Harmison)

XX XXXXX MX MXX XMXX MX MX MX MX MXM XMX MX MX MX MX M XM XXX MX MX MX MX MX MXM X M XMX MX

1. Riptide (from motion picture of the same name) (vocal by Bob Harmison)

2. I Hate Myself

3. Poor Girl

4. In Other Words, We're Thru (vocal by Bob Harmison)

5. Coffee In The Morning (from "Moulin Rouge")

M MX MX MX MX MX MX MCMXXM CMX MX MX MX MX MX MX MXMX MX MX MX MX MX MX MX MX MX MX NO

1. I Ain't Lazy--I'm Just Dreamin' zzzzzzzzzzzzzx (Vocal by Bob Harmison)

2. You Oughta Be In Pictures (vocal by Bob Harmison)

3. A Thousand Good Nights

4. I'm Nuts About Mutts (vocal by "Beanie" Sarjent)

5. Cocktails for Two (from "Murder At The Vanities") (vocal by Bob Harmison)

6. Emaline

7. Boulevard Of Broken Dreams (from "Moulin Rouge")

8. I Don't Care

9. "Why Do I Dream Those Dreams" "Goin' To Heaven On A Mule" (both from "Wonder Bar")

10. Nuthin' (vocal by Bob Harmison)

HAMMOND TIME[S]

HAMMOND, INDIANA, WEDNESDAY, APRIL 25, 1934.

AID LITTLE F[

...ger Is Cornered in S[t

...ed to ...olony Fete

VICTIMS OF DILLINGER GANG [

KIDNAPER OF MADURA LOOKS LIKE DILLINGER

Radio Announcer Relieved of Car At Home in Robertsdale

FIND HAMMOND WOMAN DIED OF AUTO INJURIES

Brought to St. Margaret's From Chicago Hospital —Hurt in Chicago

Issue Bookl[Shipping of

More Than Four-fifths of Entire Lake Tonnage Handled Here

LL ATTEMPT O PUSH PLAN OF FIRST LADY

NOT REVOLUTION

The gangsters of nearby Chicago were known to visit the Calumet Region. The *Hammond Times* on April 25, 1934, reported, "Kidnaper of Madura Looks like Dillinger: Two men, one of whom was said to resemble John Dillinger, America's public enemy number 1, kidnapped Mike 'Mickey' Madura Jr., radio announcer at a Robertsdale ballroom early today, as he drove his machine into the garage in the rear of his home at 1432 Roberts Avenue. Madura was released at 114th Street and Davis Avenue and the armed men sped east on 114th Street . . . Madura's machine was found wrecked on State Street near the Pennsylvania Railroad tracks in Calumet City . . . Madura is the son of the owner of Danceland ballroom." Madura and his "machine" are seen below with a streetcar in the background.

Ballrooms used a variety of novelty events to draw business, and the live turkeys raffled off at each year's Thanksgiving dance were always exciting prizes (right). When ladies won the turkeys, the gentlemen were needed and willing to help them get their turkeys home. One of the most successful Thanksgiving dances was in 1935, with 2,527 dancers in attendance, including seven turkey winners from Gary, Hammond, Whiting, East Chicago, and Chicago. Mike Madura got the turkeys from his mother's farm in Hannah, Indiana (below). Pictured are Mick Madura and his grandmother Anna Madura on her farm in 1935.

THURSDAY, FEB. 13TH

ROY WADDELL & HIS MUSIC

VALENTINE DANCE

MADURA'S DANCELAND

LEAP YEAR DANCE
Saturday, February 29th

Enjoyable promotional gifts were the boxes of candy given away at the annual Valentine's Day dance (left) and the annual Christmas dance. No one went home empty handed, as non-winners received a Danceland calendar for the new year. But no event was bigger than the annual New Year's Eve dance, which featured two big bands playing continuous music. In 1936, George Foster's Aristocrats of Swing (below) and the Charlie Hess Orchestra alternated between two stages. An upgraded sound system with a 12-tube, 30-watt amplifier and two dynamic speakers provided outstanding quality. Party favors were included, all for an admission charge of 50¢ for ladies and 80¢ for gentlemen.

"ARISTOCRAT"

GEORGE FOSTER

FULFILLING BRILLIANT DANCELAND ENGAGEMENT WITH HIS "ARISTOCRATS OF SWING" EACH TUESDAY, THURSDAY, SATURDAY AND SUNDAY NIGHTS. DISPLAYING AN ULTRA-MODERN BRAND OF MUSIC. HIS BAND IS RATED ONE OF THE FINEST IN THE MIDDLE WEST. HIS ENGAGEMENT CONCLUDES NEW YEAR'S EVE, AT WHICH TIME HIS UNIT ALTERNATES WITH CHARLIE HESS, ANOTHER DANCELAND FAVORITE

Final Dance Contest Plans
Will Be Completed Today

Officials of The Herald and Examiner World's Fair Dance Contest, and managers of the eleven ballrooms in which preliminaries and semifinals will be held, will meet today to complete their plans.

Within a few days all details will be disclosed as to when and where preliminaries and semifinals in all four divisions of this great contest will be held. Lists of trophies, medals, cash awards and world's fair trips will follow.

The week's engagement of all eight finalists at the Chicago Theater, where they be will stars of the stage show, already has been decided upon, as well as the finalists' entry in national contests at the world's fair.

THEATERS ASSIGN TIME.

The contest is being conducted in four divisions: tango or rhum-

ONE GROUP OF CONTESTANTS IN ACTION
Scene at Madura's Danceland in Herald and Examiner's dance carnival.

Semifinals in all four divisions will be held in the eleven ballrooms where preliminaries of the three nonswing divisions are to be decided. The jitterbugs will move from the theaters to the ballrooms after their preliminaries are over.

The eleven ballrooms are:

Herald Examiner
World's Fair Dance Contest

WE, the undersigned couple, amateur dancers 18 years of age or over, desire to enter The Herald and Examiner World's Fair Dance Contest as a team. We want to compete in the dance indicated by an X. Contestants may enter in only one division.

1. ☐ Tango or Rhumba. 2. ☐ Fox-trot. 3. ☐ Waltz.
4. ☐ Swing group (this includes shag, rug-cutting, jitterbug, Lambeth walk, etc.)

☐ Lady's Name ....
Address ....

The *Herald and Examiner* World's Fair Dance Contest held its preliminaries and semifinals at 11 ballrooms in Chicago and Indiana, including Madura's Danceland in late 1938 (above). The amateur dancers competed in the tango or rumba, fox trot, waltz, or swing division. The four winning teams received prizes and a trip to the New York World's Fair to compete for the world's championship. Other enjoyable events were leap-year dances, which were celebrated with reversed gender roles. Every man received three rings upon entering Danceland, which the ladies would earn when they requested a dance. At 11:00 p.m. the rings were counted, and the woman with the most rings received a prize of a silver ring with an ornamental mounting of a stone.

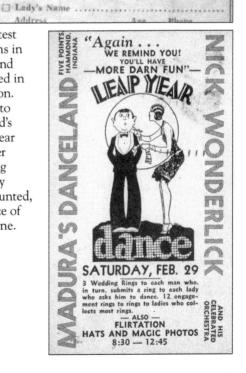

The annual Halloween masquerade was the second largest event of every year. Patrons dressed in costume and marched in the Masked Ball. Judges awarded cash prizes for the most extravagant costumes. Another event was the Straw Vote Dance held on election years. On October 19, 1940, each dancer was presented a ballot to vote for either Wendell Willkie or Franklin Roosevelt for U.S. president. At regular intervals the returns were broadcast, and prizes were awarded to those who guessed the nearest number of votes by which the victorious candidate won. Regardless of the event, Danceland was the place to go for fun. It is a well-known fact that most marriages in the region began as a dance there.

Five

THE BEST BANDS
IN THE LAND

The zenith of Madura's Danceland was from 1937 to 1942, when it featured more name bands than at any other time. Top bands of this extraordinary time in history and their corresponding pay included Paul Whiteman ($1,000), Fletcher Henderson ($450), Jack Denny ($500), Don Bestor ($500), Erskine Hawkins ($500), Mike Riley ($300), Henry Busse ($625), Lou Breese ($300), Clyde McCoy ($450), Jimmy Dorsey ($650), Glen Gray and the Casa Loma Orchestra ($800), Little Jack Little ($335), Art Kassel ($350), Joe Venuti ($200), Blue Barron ($550), Joe Sanders ($225), and Del Courtney ($400), in chronological order of appearance. These bands were paid less than at Chicago venues because Danceland was often a secondary performance for them. Other luminaries included Jack Russell, Mickey Prindl, Mark Fisher, Lee Bennett, Emil Flindt, Rita Rio, Earl Mellen, Horace Henderson, Tiny Hill, Don Pedro, Barney Rapp, Segar Ellis, Jimmy Joy, Emerson Gill, Ada Leonard, Don Ragan, Ray Pearl, Garwood Van, Val Grayson, Gray Gordon, Stepin' Fetchit, Russ Carlyle, and Jackie Coogan.

Madura's Danceland featured a rich mixture of national name bands, Chicago-based name bands, "sweet" as well as swing bands, both black and white bands, all-male and all-female bands, and "territory" bands. Gunther Schuller explained in *The Swing Era* that while the territory bands did not enjoy a national reputation, they were an integral and unique part of the era. In fact, Midwestern dancers spent more time dancing to territory bands than to name bands. And because they tended to play at a particular venue numerous times, they worked to please the clientele in order to stay employed there. In the Calumet Region in particular, every territory band's library included several polkas because of the Polish and Slovak ethic makeup of the dancing public. It is interesting to note that name band members started out as a territory musicians.

Michael J. Madura Jr. and Henrietta P. Kaminski were married on June 9, 1937, at St. Joseph's Church on Hohman Avenue in Hammond. Because Mike had booked Paul Whiteman's appearance at Danceland for two days later, the newlyweds delayed their honeymoon to New York so that Mick could help with the big event. Henrietta knew that life with the Maduras would have its challenges, but she broke off her engagement to a nice young Polish man for Mick and the excitement at Danceland. The couple spent their wedding night at the Palmer House in Chicago, where they dined in the Empire Room to the music of violinist Ralph Ginsburgh (below). They had three children: Michael D. (b. 1938), Marcia (b. 1943), and Patrice (b. 1952).

PALMER HOUSE • CHICAGO

A HILTON HOTEL

ROBERT P. WILLIFORD, GENERAL MANAGER

The Empire Room Presents

RALPH GINSBURGH

And His Concert Ensemble

Evelyn Madura and Michael Halik (right) were unusual in that they did not meet at Danceland but at a Whiting High School dance. They were married on June 3, 1936, at Sacred Heart Church in Whiting and held their wedding reception at Danceland. They had three children: Bonnie (b. 1940), Patti (b. 1943), and Lynn (b. 1947). Doris Madura and Arthur C. Borg (below) met at Danceland, were married on May 21, 1942 at Sacred Heart Church, and also held their wedding reception at Danceland. They had one daughter, Diane (b. 1947). All of the Maduras and their children worked at Danceland.

The Paul Whiteman Orchestra appeared on Friday, June 11, 1937, and made $1,000, which far exceeded any previous band pay at Danceland. The fact that Paul Whiteman was inebriated that evening and spent little time on stage was a disappointment to all. However, he autographed this photograph for Doris Madura (left). The back side of the photograph was then signed by the whole band (below): Don Moore (trumpet), Bill Rank (trombone), Jimmie Brierly (vocals), Paul Whiteman (director), Vincent Pirro (piano/accordion), Charlie Teagarden (trumpet), Mike Pingatore (?) (guitar), Jack Cordaro (clarinet/saxophone), Larry Gowar (drums), Harry "Goldie" Goldfield (trumpet), Murray Cohan (clarinet/saxophone), Normal MacPherson (brass bass), Adam Fleishmann (?), Hal Matthews (trombone), and Frank Trumbauer (clarinet/alto saxophone/C melody saxophone).

Jackie Coogan (right) and his band were a huge hit at Danceland in July 1937, drawing a crowd of 2,847. He had been one of the highest paid child movie stars in Hollywood, with acting roles with Charlie Chaplin in *The Kid*, followed by *Oliver Twist*, *Circus Days*, and *Huckleberry Finn*. Coogan's Danceland show included a company of 18, including actors Don Eddy and Lillian Tours from the Columbia Pictures movie *It Happened in Hollywood* (just before it was released in September of that year), Princess Luana from *Waikiki Wedding* and *Hawaiian Nights*, and prominent screen actress Lila Lee (below, on the Danceland stage).

JACKIE COOGAN
And His Orchestra

CONSOLIDATED RADIO ARTISTS inc
NEW YORK CHICAGO CLEVELAND HOLLYWOOD DALLAS

The great arranger, leader, and pianist Fletcher Henderson and his 14-piece band played at Danceland on the very warm evening of August 19, 1937, to an audience of 2,424. His appearance was the first stop on a road tour after a long engagement at Chicago's Grand Terrace, where nightly radio broadcasts were a big boost to his popularity. His theme song was "Christopher Columbus," written by his brother Horace, and it was a national hit the night they played at Danceland. Fletcher Henderson billboards are shown at the Danceland entrance with Mike Madura on the far right (above) and the new Mrs. Henrietta Madura (below).

Lee Bennett, who was the singing star of Jan Garber's orchestra for three years, started his own band, which played at Danceland for four nights in September 1937. His band featured the singing of Judy Randall, who also appeared with the Henry Busse and Frankie Masters Bands. Lee Bennett was an NBC and WGN radio favorite.

EXTRA!　　ALL ABOUT LEE BENNETT　　EXTRA!

MADURA'S
DANCELAND
● N E W S E T T E ●

Dance Sessions Tues., Thurs., Sat. and Sun.　SEPTEMBER 1937　Mickey Madura, Editor

DANCELAND AWAITS
LEE
BENNETT
(Three Years with Jan Garber)

—and his—
ORCHESTRA
WITH

JUDY RANDALL

In Person!　　*Four Glorious Nights!*

THURSDAY, SEPT. 2nd First Nighters Greet Lee, Et Al

SATURDAY, SEPT. 4th "Circle Dance" 10:30-11:00 Dance Till 12:30

SUNDAY, SEPT. 5th "Waltz Night" Every 3rd Dance in Three-Quarter Time

—And Let's All Celebrate—

*Monday, Sept. 6th—Labor Day

*The Special Dance for Which Lee Bennett Was Especially Engaged

SORRY, BUT JACK RUSSELL SAYS
AU REVOIR SUNDAY, AUG. 29

MCA.
JACK RUSSELL
and his
MARVELOUS N B C ORCHESTRA

Jack Russell led a very popular Chicago orchestra, which appeared at Madura's Danceland for a week in August 1937. Featured at the 1933 Chicago World's Fair, the band was often booked at the famous Aragon and Trianon Ballrooms and enjoyed a long residency at the Melody Mill Ballroom.

GRAND STAIRWAY, ARAGON, "THE WONDER BALLROOM," 1100 LAWRENCE AVENUE, UPTOWN CHICAGO

The Aragon (above), Trianon, and Melody Mill (below) were the most beautiful ballrooms in the city of Chicago and provided healthy competition and new ideas for the Maduras. The Aragon Ballroom was located approximately 5 miles north of downtown Chicago. Built in 1926, it had a Spanish theme and attracted the best of the name big bands in the era. The Trianon Ballroom opened in 1922 on the South Side of Chicago. Decorated in Louis XVI elegance, it competed with the Aragon for the best big bands. The Melody Mill Ballroom opened in 1931 with the Jack Russell Orchestra.

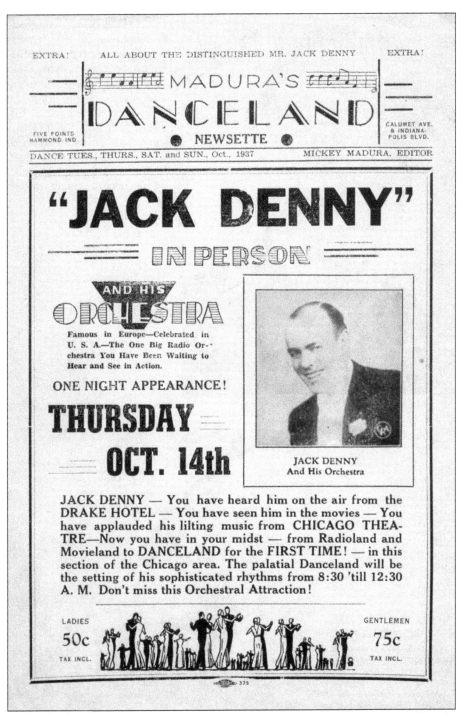

Jack Denny, one of the all-around best dance bands featured at the Drake Hotel, the Chicago Theatre, the Waldorf-Astoria Hotel, and the Hotel Pierre, appeared at Danceland on Thursday, October 14, 1937. His band was equally at home with sweet-style and hot swing–style music. Denny's unique arrangements featured no brass—just strings (including harp, electric steel guitar and two pianos), woodwinds, and novel percussion instruments, including the celesta.

During Don Bestor's engagement on November 18, 1937, his trumpet player was arrested by Whiting policemen for not paying child support, but he returned to play after his ex-father-in-law paid a $2,000 real estate bond for his release from jail. Bestor's theme songs were "I'm Not Forgetting" and "Teach Me to Smile." Jack Benny hired the Bestor Orchestra for his successful radio show.

A popular dance band appearing in March 1938 was that of Erskine Hawkins, who was often billed as "The 20th-Century Gabriel." After studying at State Teachers College in Alabama, he became the leader of the school band and toured extensively. He composed his band's theme song, "Tuxedo Junction," with band members Julian Dash and William Johnson.

WINCHELL SAYS: "An orchid to Erskine Hawkins' torrid trumpeting—definitely the best I've ever hard."

SULLIVAN SAYS: "It is my contention that Hawkins is the greatest of them all, and that includes Armstrong."

ERSKINE HAWKINS

"HI, KIDS!"

EMIL FLINDT

The dean of America's maestri who returns to "The Land o' Dance" July 4th for an indefinite stay. "Pops" has two sons in his band now but is still the boss.

GOTTA WEAR TIES, BOYS

It is a cardinal rule at Madura's Danceland that our gentlemen wear neckties on all shirts — sport or otherwise. It not only looks very neat but you can't top that well-dressed feeling of confidence when you ask a girl for a dance. The ladies wouldn't like you in a sweaty polo shirt all wrinkled-up. Men, there's nothing like a clean white dress shirt with a neatly tied necktie.

Moreover, to dance sans suitcoats the shirts must have long sleeves that mustn't be rolled up. Suspenders are out, too, when dancing without a coat.

Smoking is permitted at Madura's Danceland on the promenade, and that's something that will keep you cool under the collar. Another way to keep cool, adhere to "straight-dancing." Besides, too much fancy stepping might draw a tap on your shoulder from someone asking you to stop rocking-the-boat. Any conspicuous kind of dancing here is taboo. Play safe — keep cool — "straight-dance!"

Some 7,000 people broke attendance records to hear Emil Flindt and his 13-piece band restart the radio broadcasts on WIND on January 20, 1938. Mick Madura noted the process of the remote broadcast, "Emil calls WIND via a special phone located in the back of the band-shell. The warning signal to begin the broadcast is two short rings followed in one minute by one long ring, which means we're on the air." The "platinum-haired maestro" (right) composed the theme song of Wayne King, "The Waltz You Saved for Me," while serving in the war in France. He had dedicated it to the drivers of the army trucks and originally titled it "The Truck Driver's Dream." The Danceland billboard (below) advertises the bands of Emil Flindt and Ken Nowlan.

63

The Hollywood Ingenues (above) played a 1938 Memorial Day dance at Danceland. Their saxophonist and former Whiting girl, Alyce Plise, was greeted by Mayor McNamara and city attorney McCarthy with a bouquet of flowers. Plise had spent 10 months with the Ziegfeld Follies and had performed in 28 nations. She was married to Ray Fabing, the leader of the band.

Emil Velazco's 10-piece band was so popular with the Danceland crowd that it broke the Sunday record for attendance with 3,200 dancers. Velazco played a $20,000 portable organ and was known especially for the "grab bag," which inspired community singing on tunes such as "The Music Goes 'Round 'n 'Round," "Yes, We Have No Bananas," and "Barney Google."

The year 1938 was an active one for business (right). Mick Madura noted, "In 1938 we had one-nighters, name-bands, increased prices, and lavish attractions" with a net profit of more than $11,000. The Jimmy Dorsey Orchestra performed at Danceland on September 16 with vocalist Bob Eberle following a six-week engagement at the Bon Air Country Club in Wheeling, Illinois. Jimmy Dorsey was a virtuoso alto saxophonist and clarinetist, and his band's theme song featured his saxophone-playing on "Contrasts." Other Dorsey recorded hits of the time were "Beebe," "Sandman," "Hollywood Pastime," "It's the Dreamer in Me," "Parade of the Milk Bottle Caps," and "Flight of the Bumble Bee." The burned edges of the Jimmy Dorsey window card (below) are from the 1967 Danceland fire.

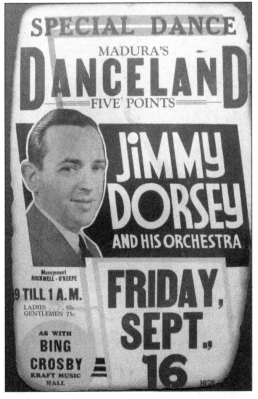

RITA RIO NEXT

Rita Rio and her 12 Rhythm Girls played at Danceland on September 10, 1938. Rio, who excelled at singing, dancing, and directing the band, hailed from Miami, Florida. She was discovered by Samuel Goldwyn, who whisked her off to Hollywood to work with Eddie Cantor in *Strike Me Pink*. She later became the movie star Dona Drake.

danceland
presents
A
NEW STAR
●
Earl Mellen
His Orchestra
●

"*melodies by mellen*"

FIVE brilliant dancing dates with the **Treat of the Season** are ours Sat., Feb. 18, Sun. 19, Thurs. 23, Sat. 25 and Sun. 26! "Melodies by Mellen," the by-line by which Earl Mellen's orchestra is known from coast-to-coast, is coming from recent triumphs at the Cavalier Hotel and Beach Club in Virginia Beach, Virginia; and Bill Green's Casino in Pittsburg, Pa., where Earl Mellen was a Mutual Network feature twice nightly. Earl Mellen presents strictly a youthful band, a nifty combination of talented artistry and handsome masculinity, a unit that is certain to be as much admired by the men as by the girls. Critics call Mellen's tempo, contagious.

Earl Mellen, en route to Kansas City, stops over five nights

Earl Mellen led a youthful 12-piece band for five nights in February 1939. The traveling band had most recently performed at the Cavalier Hotel and Beach Club in Virginia Beach, Virginia, and Bill Green's Casino in Pittsburgh, Pennsylvania. They were heading to Kansas City after their stop at Madura's Danceland.

The band of "Tiny" Hill (who was 6 feet tall and 330 pounds) achieved notoriety in 1938 with broadcasts over WGN from the Melody Mill Ballroom in Chicago. Hill sold more than 100,000 copies of his Vocalion Records hits "Angry," "Doodle Dee Doo," and "Mama's Gone Good-Bye." The Tiny Hill Orchestra was contracted to play a two-week engagement at Danceland in early December 1939, which was then extended through mid-February 1940 to include the Christmas Night, New Year's Eve, and President Roosevelt Balls. Hill's singers included Irwin Bendel, as well as the left-handed bass player and scat singer Pat Patterson.

When the cameraman caught our 350-pound Danceland Maestro, "Tiny" Hill, he was in the middle of his famous revival, "Angry." Cancelation of Ray Jones' Band made it possible to hold-over "Tiny" Hill indefinitely on Thursdays, Saturdays, Sundays and Holidays.

MADURA'S

DANCELAND

5 POINTS · INDANAPOLIS BLVD. & 114 ST · RTS. 12 · 20 · 41

Newsette

Mickey Madura, Editor   FEBRUARY 1, 1941   Official Danceland Organ

JOE VENUTI

SWING		AND HIS
KING		WORLD
OF THE		FAMOUS
FIDDLE		BAND

Not One -- But 2 Grand Nites

NEXT SAT. & SUN.
JAN. 18 & 19

Joe Venuti, known as "The Swing King of the Fiddle," brought his 14-piece orchestra, including singer Kay Starr, to Madura's Danceland January 18–19, 1941. Venuti played in Paul Whiteman's band for eight years before forming his own group. He was born Giuseppe Venuti to Italian parents aboard a ship in the middle of the Atlantic Ocean, began playing violin at the age of four, and later studied with Thaddeus Rich of the Philadelphia Orchestra. He played a variety of styles of music and was known for his sense of humor, impersonations, and daring nature. His orchestra played at the Belmont Plaza Hotel, State Theatre, and Roseland Ballroom of New York, the Ocean Park Casino in Hollywood, on NBC and CBS commercial programs, and in the Warner Brothers movie *Garden of the Moon*. His theme song was an original composition titled "Last Night."

Thurs., May 15

ONE NITE ONLY

MCA PRESENTS
•
IN PERSON
•
THE NATION'S
FAVORITE
MUSIC MAN
•
BROADCASTING
COAST to COAST
NBC · CBS
•
COMPOSER
OF
"HELL'S BELLS"
•
SEE HIM
AND
HIS MERRY
GANG

ART KASSEL
AND HIS
Kassels in the Air

Dancing Till
12:30
LADIES - 40c
GENTS - 50c
PLUS TAX

With MARION HOLMES — CUB HIGGINS
HARVEY CRAWFORD, ET AL
—— featuring ——
"Alexander Was a Swoose"
"Just Around the Corner," Etc.

MADURA'S
DANCELAND

Two great bands appeared at Danceland in May 1941. Art Kassel (right) was born in Chicago, and his Kassels in the Air Orchestra recorded on Bluebird, Columbia, and Victor Records. Their theme songs were "Doodle Doo Doo" and "Hell's Bells." James Maloney (below) became a hit at Joyland Park in Galveston, Texas, and adopted the name Jimmy Joy. His claim to fame was his ability to play two clarinets at the same time. His singers included Art London, Betty Burns, and the Joy Vocal Trio, Quartet, and Quintet; he featured a five-part harmony Joy Sax Section. Their theme song was "Shine On, Harvest Moon."

Home of America's Finest Floor

Madura's **DANCELAND NEWSETTE**

MICKEY MADURA, Editor   MAY, 1941

MARTHA REAL (
Martha Nash, a g
ndeed, as we see h
ay night, is really a
lla girl. And proud
finds her quite a cor
er's helper with t
Martha's way of re
all. Then at night,
a magic wand has
g amorous again. A
only Martha can —
mythical Cinderella

ART KASSEL (

DANCE *with* **JOY** SUN. MAY **4**

JIMMY JOY BRINGS ACE HOLLYWOOD BAND TO BALLROOM FOR ONE NIGHT

Jimmy Joy, who brings his famous band to Madura's on Sunday (Only One Nite), May 4th, thru arrangements with MCA, signs his checks "James Monte Maloney."

Jimmy Joy became such a tremendous hit at Joyland Park, Galveston, Texas, a few seasons ago where, because he was a constant "hold over," his name became synonomous with the park. So he naturally dropped "Maloney," and pinned on "Joy." People have been "Dancing with Joy" ever since.

Coast-to-coast, the name Jimmy Joy is a magnate

Many variables contributed to a dance band's popularity and reception at Danceland, including the night of the week the band performed, the band's stage of development, the audience's familiarity with the band, and even the weather (above, trolleys running during a snowstorm) and religious holidays (Lent in the Roman Catholic community could be particularly devastating to business). These variables occasionally accounted for low attendance for some well-paid name bands or for a capacity crowd for a local favorite who knew the dispositions of the dancers. One favorite territory bandleader from the 1937–1938 years was Kay Jones (below).

MUSIC THAT APPEALS—Kay Jones and His Orches-   Group Photograph.   A Rare September Treat for Ro-
tra with Lovely Edith Klyde, who will Command Danc-   mantic September Dancing is Kay Jones—A Most Wel-
ing at Danceland on Four Occasions Announced Above   come Newcomer in th "LAND OF DANCE."

MADURA'S DANCELAND NEWSETTE

MICKEY MADURA, Editor   OCTOBER, 1939   Indpls., Calumet & 114th——5 Points

PRESENTING PAUL PAGE

Baritone singer Paul Page and his band came from the North Side of Chicago, and their "sweet" style was enjoyed by the Danceland crowd. One especially favorite bandleader was Eddie Camden. Other bandleaders included Layton Bailey, Ralph Barlow, Howard Becker, Rudy Bundy, Vincent Burns, Dewey Cass, Dick Cisne, "Doc" Clayton, Jack Conrad, Freddie Daw, Eddie Dunsmoor, Ted Earl, Joe Gerken, Emerson Gill, Dick Gordon, Glen Gordon, Joe Hart, Charlie Hess, Noel Howell, Mickey Isley, Jimmie Jackson (with then unknown singer Perry Como), Johnny Kay, Henry Kayner, Johnny Long, Mary Marshall, Ray Maxon, Mac McCloud, Ed McGraw, Carlos Molina, Hal Moore, Bill Munday, Red Nering, Ernie Palmquist, Karl Parker, Rex Paul, Bob Phillips, Bill Pryer, Mike Riley, Red Roberts, George Rusch, Billy Scott, Johnny Sisul, Chuck Swanson, Ozzie Thrane, Palmer Whitney, Art Wilson, Woody Wilson, Terry York, and Eddie Young.

The admission ticket from the 1930s (above) reflects the early style of letterhead stationery used at Madura's Danceland. The second style (below) was used until the end of the Danceland era for all formal correspondence, including contracts. Interestingly enough, the location is indicated on the first style as Hammond, Indiana, and on the second as Whiting, Indiana. This ambiguity of the official location of Five Points exists to this day. The thin stretch of northwestern-most Indiana land sandwiched between Wolf Lake and Whiting is officially Hammond but uses Whiting mailing addresses.

Six

WORLD WAR II
AND THE BUSINESS

World War II had its beginnings in 1939 when Hitler invaded Poland, but the United States did not enter the war until late 1941. However, on June 10, 1940, Italy declared war on France and Great Britain, and Pres. Franklin Roosevelt, elected to his third term that year, broadcast on radio the promise of material support for both countries. Coincidentally, the trolley cars that had long brought patrons to Five Points were permanently stopped on the day before, June 9. And on July 4, the Maduras began paying a defense tax of 10 percent on ballroom profits, raising admission that same amount. No one knew what was coming on December 7, 1941, "A date which will live in infamy" according to Roosevelt, when the Japanese Navy bombed Pearl Harbor, killing 2,433 Americans and wounding 1,178.

Mick Madura's *Newsette* provided perspective on World War II and its effect on the dance business. The January 1942 newsletter contains multiple references to the war, with messages such as "Buy U.S. Bonds and Stamps," "Send *Newsettes* to Our Boys in Camps," and "Special Weekend Price for Servicemen." It advertised Danceland's ideal central location for short drives "because of the acute tire and fuel rationing that prevails," its low admission fee of 30¢ and 40¢, and the importance of entertainment in keeping morale high.

Many bands broke up during the war, especially when the leader or key players were drafted. Before the war, there were more than 21,000 dance orchestras in the United States involving more than 100,000 musicians. By the summer of 1942, most of the name bands had lost at least a quarter of their musicians, seriously harming the big band industry.

After many successful years, there was a lull in business when the men went into the armed services, and the women also stopped coming. After 14 years of being open for business every Tuesday, Thursday, Saturday, and Sunday, Danceland canceled its famous Thursday night dances.

An extra 1,000 copies of *Newsette* were printed in August 1941 "for the Danceland boys in training for Uncle Sam although they probably won't get to see Blue Barron on Danceland's 12th Anniversary." The Blue Barron Orchestra (above) played on August 16 and featured Russ Carlyle, Charlie Fisher, Ronnie Snyder, and the Three Blue Notes. "The Music of Yesterday and Today Styled the Blue Barron Way" referred to their arrangements, which merged the first few measures of an old song with a new one. Blue Barron recorded the songs "Heart and Soul," "I Married an Angel," and "Spring Is Here." Other bandleaders who appeared from 1941 to 1944 were Johnny Gilbert (right), Russ Bothe, Larry Conti, Edgar Drake, Bill Funkey, Al Graham, Teddy Harris, Bob Helm, Walley Humphrey, Augie Knapp, Don Lang, Johnny Marlow, Ted Nering, and Johnny Raptis.

Ada Leonard's 17-piece all-female orchestra, with star trumpet soloist Jane Sager, performed on United Service Organizations (USO) tours between 1940 and 1942 and appeared at Danceland September 27–28, 1941. Sager, known as the "high-note doctor," had also played in Rita Rio's band, which later hired Ada Leonard (pictured), a former burlesque queen. Sager was an immeasurable help to Leonard in the success of her band. Ken Shirk, previously of radio station WIND but then serving in the Canal Zone, wrote the following postcard to Mick Madura, dated October 10, 1941, regarding the appearance of Ada Leonard's band, "Why didn't you have things like this when I was at WIND? I would have been over to check the radio equipment every night. It is too hot to do much dancing here, and the Panama government requires the bands to play half Latin-American music. See you when the 'war' is over."

President Roosevelt requested the playing of the national anthem before and after every event, and on Christmas night 1941, Johnny Knopp was the first band to comply. New Year's Eve featured Commissioner Dave Cunningham and the Midshipmen Orchestra (pictured). Their theme song was "Anchors Aweigh." Madura's *Newsette* reminded patrons that "no more tin or lead foil on cigarettes will be used after March 15."

The "Bomb Boogie" was a new jitterbug creation that was photographed at Danceland in March 1943 at a dance for war workers from the Pullman-Standard plant in Hammond. Each Saturday, Pullman staged an all-night dance so that all the shift workers would have time to relax. Del Courtney was the band that entertained audiences that wartime night.

Tickets for "Remember Pearl Harbor" Club Dance

Forty-one women volunteered to sell tickets and act as hostesses for the "Remember Pearl Harbor" knitting club dance at Danceland on April 17, 1942. They were, from left to right, Harriet Dudleston, Genevieve Martin, Wanda Polk, Donna Archer, Ellen Vezmer, Shirley Monihan, Marjory Schultz, Annette Kolodziej, Sue Domsic, Helen Domsic, Anne Mrezar, Ilene Girman, Nora Driscoll, Margaret Hladeck, Joyce Kowalski, Emma Kordula, Adeline Bodney, Rose Butkovich, Elsie Hayes, Doris Bukivch, Jane Hopper, Joyce Wargo, Madelyn Schaefer, Rosellen Thwing, Jeanne Bates, Mary Duhon, Helen Vrbancic, Eileen De Jerf, Lois Hildebrandt, Yvonne Bareska, and Josephine Pihulic. Those unseen are Julia Dykiel, Catherine Barid, Wanda Eley, Army Hammond, Betty Kiekenapp, Wanda Lark, Angela Celano, Carolyn Graham, Dorothy Pickett, and Juliann Kulik. Some 2,000 women had knitted 500 sweaters for the soldiers away from home, and thank-you notes were received from as far away as Pearl Harbor, Alaska, Iceland, Guam, and the Canal Zone.

The band that played for the Remember Pearl Harbor dance was that of Bill Keulbs, pictured here at Madura's Danceland. Buses brought three loads of servicemen from Chicago, who joined others from the Calumet Region in the festivities. Sixty women and their servicemen-escorts formed a huge "V" for victory and sang the national anthem and "God Bless America."

This 3¢ "Win the War" U.S. postage stamp was issued on July 4, 1942, to give a boost to American morale during the dark days of World War II and to symbolize the nation's goal of victory. During World War II, the U.S. government issued over 25 different postage stamps with war-related images. (Courtesy of David Ward-Steinman.)

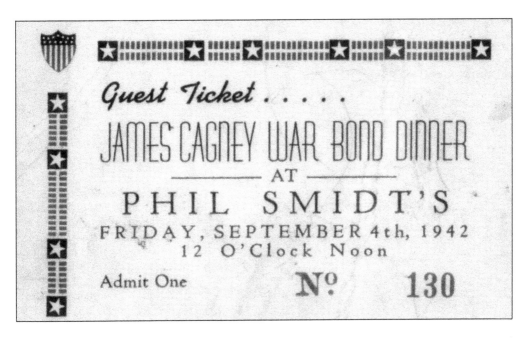

Guest Ticket . . . . .

JAMES CAGNEY WAR BOND DINNER

— AT —

PHIL SMIDT'S

FRIDAY, SEPTEMBER 4th, 1942
12 O'Clock Noon

Admit One   № 130

Times were tense during the war years. Mick Madura noted that people were impatient and required intense types of entertainment from high-action or ridiculously funny movies to eccentric dances. To ease some tension, the city of Whiting held the James Cagney War Bond Dinner at Phil Smidt's restaurant on September 4, 1942. Cagney had won the Academy Award for Best Actor that year for his portrayal of George M. Cohan in "Yankee Doodle Dandy" and spent 1942 volunteering to entertain war audiences. Mick Madura met the great actor and keynote speaker there and requested his autograph.

Mick Madura was drafted into the army at the age of 33, leaving wife Henrietta home with their small children, Michael D. and Marcia. Pvt. Michael J. Madura (left) was stationed at Fort Knox, Kentucky (below), and Fort Ord, California. His absence from Danceland during this time resulted in the dissolution of the *Newsette* until after his return to civilian life in October 1946. These war years marked a decline in nights open for business due to so many men away at war, midnight curfews, and tire and gas rationing. Mileage rationing records were issued for each application for gasoline.

Tank in Armored Force Division, Fort Knox, Ky.

Henrietta Madura is pictured here (right) writing a letter to Mick, who was serving in the U.S. Army. The family used war ration books (below) containing stamps for purchasing "goods in the quantities and at the times designated by the Office of Price Administration." Printed in each ration book were guidelines that read, "Rationing is a vital part of your war effort. Any effort to violate the rules is an effort to deny someone his share and will create hardship and help the enemy. This book is your Government's assurance of your right to buy your fair share of certain goods made scarce by war. . . . Give your whole support to rationing and thereby conserve our vital goods. Be guided by the rule: *If you don't need it, DON'T BUY IT.*"

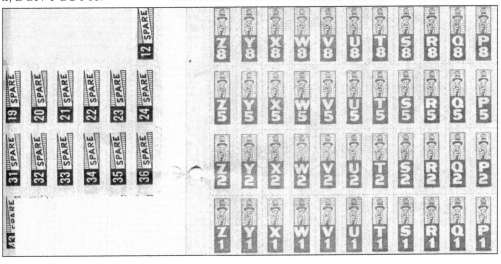

COMPLIMENTARY TICKET

STUDENT MIXER

•

MADURA'S DANCELAND

375

MADURA'S
DANCELAND
★ ★

JOHNNY KNOPP
and his MUSICAL TOP
Orchestra

DANCE AND STAY YOUNG!

In 1943, Danceland began holding student mixers every other Friday night after the high school football games to bring students from all of the local schools together. From 1943 through 1945, few name bands were featured at Danceland, while more territory bands appeared. Pianist Johnny Knopp (left), who first played at Danceland in 1937, enjoyed several extended stays. Territory band pay ranged from $70 to $90. These were lean years for the Madura family until World War II ended in 1945. Because of Mick Madura's absence from Danceland during his army service years, there are no archived materials for this time period.

Seven

POSTWAR DANCELAND

The postwar years of 1946 to 1950 showed a resurgence in the number of name bands performing at Danceland. Several appeared through the management of MCA, and they included Blue Barron, Clyde McCoy, Ted Weems, Benny Strong, Orrin Tucker, George Olsen, Tiny Hill, Griff Williams, Sherman Hayes, and Will Back. Between 1947 and 1950, the following bands performed and were paid the indicated amount: Harry Cool ($450), Ray Anthony ($500), Griff Williams ($650), Russ Morgan ($1,000), Al Trace ($650), Gene Krupa ($650) Vaughn Monroe ($2,500), and Tex Beneke. During this period, the pay of territory bands kept pace with the rising cost of living, ranging from $100 to $150 per night.

Upon Mick Madura's return home from the army, he resurrected the monthly patron newsletters in April 1947 under the new name of the *Ballroom Encore* and began using the pen name of Leahcim Arudam (Michael Madura spelled backwards). He reported that dancing was held on Tuesdays, Saturdays, and Sundays from 8:00 p.m. until midnight for a general admission price of 60¢. Danceland kept the nine-year tradition of Ladies' Night on Tuesdays, with admission remaining 30¢ before 8:00 p.m. He changed the name of the newsletter again for a few months in 1948 and 1949 to the *Evening Star* in time for Madura's Danceland's 20-year anniversary. But by April of that year, he returned it to its original 1933 and classic name, *Newsette*, because after two years of new names "the dancers insist on calling this little newspaper *Newsette*."

WELCOME GRIFF

After the war, Danceland featured instruction by the Fred Astaire Studios of Hammond and Gary and continued to be rented out to private clubs, schools, churches, and unions for dances and catered banquets. Pianist Griff Williams (left) was hired to play for the 25th anniversary celebration of Local 395, International Association of Bridge, Structural, and Ornamental Iron Workers, whose first president was Mike Madura. A line of happy people stretched for two blocks to enter Danceland (below).

Singer, saxophonist, and arranger Sherman Hayes brought his orchestra to Madura's Danceland on Decoration Day in 1947. Having worked with the bands of Del Courtney, George Olsen, and Orville Knapp and in the 20th Century Fox studios, he later organized his own band. His theme song and radio hit was "Cuddle Up a Little Closer."

"It's Cool in November!" refers to the appearance of singer and bandleader Harry Cool on November 20, 1947. He sang for three years over WGN with the Dick Jurgens Orchestra with hits such as "A Million Dreams Ago" and "Why Don't You Fall in Love with Me." As director of the Carl Ravazza Band, he recorded on Mercury Records.

The all-time favorite territory band at Madura's Danceland was that of saxophonist and vocalist Johnny Kay (left) from East Chicago. Kay's band set a record in 1947 for performing there more than any other ensemble, appearing in 38 different months since their opening on New Year's Eve 1942. Following Kay's all-time record was Mickey Isley, with both bands having played at Danceland regularly until 1959. Other popular territory bandleaders during 1947 were Mickey Prindl and Will Back (below). In a *Newsette* that year, Mick Madura reminded the patrons of the long-held house policy of "no jitterbugging at Danceland."

MCA *Presents* IN PERSON!

WILL BACK AND HIS FAMOUS ORCHESTRA

SPARKLING RHYTHM!

TOP FLIGHT ENTERTAINMENT!

The 20th anniversary of Madura's Danceland in 1949 was celebrated by featuring many great bands that year. "The first 20 years are the hardest," quipped Mike Madura (pictured), then 61 years old. "It was pretty hard keeping open during the war years, but when the boys came home they were really happy we hadn't closed. Treat them right, and they'll treat you right."

This aerial view of Five Points and beyond was taken in 1949 by Mercury Photography. The famous intersection of Indianapolis Boulevard, Calumet Avenue, and 114th Street is located at the bottom, just left of center. Margaret's Geneva House is at the bottom center, with Madura's Danceland directly to the right of it. The large white building further to the right is Phil Smidt's restaurant, with the Lever Brothers factory across the street.

RAY ANTHONY, whose brilliant young orchestra comes to town for a one night engagement direct from New York Anthony, one of the brightest young stars in music, sings and plays trumpet.

the talk ✶
✶ of America ✶
Ray ANTHONY
AND HIS ✶
✶ ORCHESTRA

20th Jubilee Feb. 24

The 20th anniversary of Danceland was first celebrated on February 24, 1949, with trumpeter Ray Anthony and his 21-piece orchestra, which was considered one of the best bands in the United States. Only 27 years old, Anthony had already led a navy band, the Dolphins, in several Pacific outposts after having played in both the Glenn Miller and Jimmy Dorsey Orchestras. He drew a large crowd of college students from the University of Chicago and Indiana and Purdue Universities. Less than one month after his Danceland appearance, Anthony was signed to Capitol Records. His hit songs included "Harbor Lights," "At Last," and "The Bunny Hop" (below), "Peter Gunn," and "Dragnet."

how to do the bunny hop

TEMPO—4 beats to the bar

1. Stand with feet together

2. Right foot out to side, bring back. Repeat.

3. Left foot out to side, bring back. Repeat.

4. 1 hop forward with feet together

5. 1 hop back to starting position with feet together

6. 3 hops forward

Bunny Hop (congal line) can be formed with hands on shoulders or hips.

The 20-year anniversary of Danceland was celebrated next with the 18-piece band of pianist Frankie Carle on March 10, 1949. Frankie Carle (right) featured his daughter, Marjorie Hughes, who sang his 1949 top-10 release "Cruising Down the River on a Sunday Afternoon." Carle's first no. 1 hit recording was "Oh! What It Seemed to Be," followed by "Rumors Are Flying," "It's All Over Now," and "Roses in the Rain," all sung by Hughes. Carle was first recognized with the Horace Heidt band, and he then started his own band in 1943. The photograph from Danceland's stage shows (below, from left to right) Mick Madura, Tom Piljac, Frankie Carle, and Mike Madura.

DANCELAND AWAITS FRANKIE CARLE

THURS. MAR. 10
TILL 12:30

Frankie Carle...The one and only! Yessiree, it's "thee" Frankie Carle, in person...coming out Indianapolis Blvd. way...Thursday March 10th...Eighteen (18) people...One is Marjorie Hughes, Frankie's own daughter...a star in her own right...Plus Twin Pianos...and the program won't be over until 12:30.

An exclusive engagement for which Frankie Carle receives $3500 per hour...Our best Sunday crowd for one of the best of the nation's top bands..."The Golden Touch"...maker of 120,000,000 records of Sunrise Serenade, Oh, What It Seems To Be, Rumors Are Flying, Roses In the Rain, Falling Leaves, etc. Taught by his Uncle Nicholas Colangelo. Frankie has become the country's master of the keyboard... His phenomenal mark must be attributed to his knack of "playing like the people."

First became recognized with Horace Heidt...organized own band in 1943 and played first engagement at Hotel Pennsylvania in N. Y... Wanted to be a boxer...against wishes of parents who could see him only as a concert pianist...Frankie never misses a boxing match...Likes Gershwin best of all...Favorite tune is Stardust...He's 5'5" tall and weighs 142 pounds...The Golden Touch.

America's Finest Floor "Air Cushioned"

WALTZ ON SUN.
EVERY 3rd SET IN ¼ TIME

CARLE BOOGIE — FRANKIE CARLE will be the second of famous names to mark the 20th Jubilee of Madura's Danceland. The Big Date is Thursday, evening, March 10th — One Night Only — But an Exclusive One. What more could we ask? Dancers and Non-Dancers Welcome.

THE FOURSOME

The next 20th jubilee appearance was by Tex Beneke and his 24-piece Glenn Miller Band on Saturday, April 9, 1949. Glenn Miller had initially enlisted in the army in 1942 and then transferred to the air force as an assistant special services officer. On December 15, 1944, he departed on a flight to France to entertain troops that never reached its destination. Gordon "Tex" Beneke, who played tenor saxophone and sang with the Modernaires, took over the band in 1945. Some of the hits of the Glenn Miller Band under the direction of Tex were "St. Louis Blues March," "I Can Dream Can't I?," and "Cherokee Canyon." The 35-year-old Beneke and band drew a crowd that formed a line from Danceland to the corner of Five Points. The photograph below shows Mick Madura and Tex Beneke (right) shaking hands backstage.

THE MADURA'S DANCELAND NEWSETTE

TEX BENEKE WAS THE APRIL BAND-OF-THE-MONTH FOR THE 20th YEAR JUBILEE OF MADURA'S DANCELAND. TEX ATTRACTED THE CROWD-OF-THE-YEAR. THE CAMERA GIVES US A QUICK PEEK OF THE THRONG DURING THE PLAYING OF "TULSA." A WARM HANDSHAKE BETWEEN MICHAEL MADURA, JR. AND TEX SHOWS A GOOD TIME WAS HAD BY ALL.

20th JUBILEE

MADURA'S

DANCELAND

5 POINTS · INDIANAPOLIS BLVD. & 114 ST · RTS. 12 · 20 · 41

MAY 1949

Newsette

"SUNFLOWER" "CRUISING — DOWN — THE — RIVER" "SO TIRED"

MUSIC IN THE MORGAN MANNER

"DOES YOUR HEART BEAT FOR ME?"

"BARROOM POLKA"

'HIS CRYING TROMBONE'

Russ

MORGAN
and his ORCHESTRA

THURSDAY!
NIGHT
9 until 1 o'clock

MAY 19th

Another 20th jubilee band was Russ Morgan's on May 19, 1949. By age 21, Morgan had arranged for John Phillip Sousa, Victor Herbert, and Jean Goldkette. With his own band, his vocal and trombone style led to hits including "So Tired" and "Does Your Heart Beat for Me?" Mick Madura interviewed Morgan's press agent, who told him, "Best of all are one-nighters at ballrooms, theaters, and concerts. A few nights ago our band grossed $5,000 in Laredo, Texas. Big bands lose money working a hotel dining room, which spends about $2,500 a week for music, while a band like Russ's has a payroll of $3,000 a week: 19 musicians, plus a band boy, secretary, lawyer, booking agent, press agent, and road manager. However, bands use the hotel's broadcast to great advantage. On a network program, our band becomes known in almost every town, and that's where our future one-nighter bookings are. Yet after a hard grind of one-nighters, it's nice to end up at another hotel where we can catch up, refresh our wardrobe, and see the Doc about our ulcers!"

Henry "Hot Lips" Busse (left) was the 20th jubilee anniversary band on October 14, 1949. Busse was born in Holland, came to the United States playing in a ship's band, and gained renown on trumpet in Paul Whiteman's orchestra. His own ensemble got its start on Cincinnati radio and then moved to Chicago and Hollywood. Busse is known for his use of mutes, for his shuffle rhythm, and through his composition and opening theme song "Hot Lips" and closing theme "When Day is Done." Chicago-based bandleader Al Trace also appeared in 1949. Trace is best known for two of his 300 compositions, "Mairzy Doats" (below) and "If I Knew You Were Coming I'd've Baked a Cake."

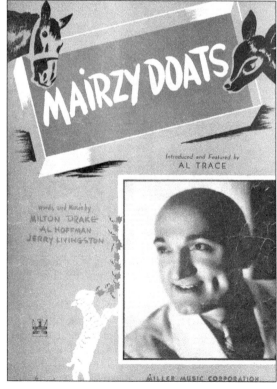

The year 1950 was memorable for the successful one-night engagements of two big name bands. Russ Morgan, who was paid $1,000, brought in over 2,000 people on April 15, and Vaughn Monroe and his Camel Caravan played to 3,414 patrons on April 20, for which they were paid $2,500. Monroe's 26-piece orchestra included violinist Earl Hummel, impressionist Jay Lawrence, harmonica player Dick Hyman, Ziggy Talent, and the Moon Maids and Men. His hit recordings included "Requestfully Yours," "There! I've Said It Again," "I Wish I Didn't Love You So," and his theme song, "Racing with the Moon." Morgan and Monroe were the only name bands of 1950, while the regular house bands were led by Roy Milton and Mickey Prindl.

1950 in Review at MADURA DANCELAND

Vaughn Monroe Scored Biggest Nite

1950 will long be remembered as the year Vaughn Monroe played here. To be exact it was Thursday, April 20, only 5 days after Russ Morgan's Danceland visit.

Vaughn's was well-received by the 3414 persons who paid $2.00 per ticket to see him and his orchestra of 26 artists, including Ziggy Talent, Jay Lawrence, the Moon Maids and the Moon Men. It was Jay Lawrence impressionist, whose encore applause rivaled his bosses. Mainly Monroe's dance music was Rythmic and Dance. Compelling. Photos at right show part of crowd.

RUSS MORGAN'S 1950 one-nighter on Saturday, April 15 topped his own 1949 engagement at Madura's by far. Russ' trade mark "Music in the Morgan Manner" was enhanced by his brilliant trombone work. Russ, as always emphasized dance ability rather than show work. Russ' crowd was over the 2000 mark.

Those were the only two name bands to appear here. However, during the month of August and part of September for six weeks our regular night patrons were treated to a guest singing star in Roy Milton's orchestra. He was Eddie Carr who won the Harvest moon Festival under the name of Kyle Kimbrough and now is on daily Television programs.

Another regular star looms at Madura's. He is Mickey Prindl, whose orchestra is receiving high praise from critics as a "National Favorite Prospect."

The great drummer Gene Krupa was born in South Chicago in 1909 of Polish immigrant parents. In 1934, he recorded "Sing, Sing, Sing" with the Benny Goodman Orchestra and played with many stars, including Anita O'Day, Roy Eldridge, and Tommy Dorsey. He is credited with highlighting the drummer and drum solo and recording the first studio jazz disc to feature bass drum and tom-toms. Krupa's own big band opened and closed 1951 at Danceland and featured his playing on "Dark Eyes," "Lover," and "How High the Moon" and Wild Bill Davison's cornet on "Bonaparte's Retreat." In his 1990 book *Drummin' Men*, Bert Korall sums up Krupa's playing as "swing, charm, facility, and authority. Krupa creates an ambiance that is his alone." Mick Madura went to Krupa's funeral in Chicago and saved the remembrance card pictured below.

In Loving Memory of

Gene B. Krupa

Born, January 15, 1909
At Rest, October 16, 1973

Services Saturday, Oct. 20, 1973
Immaculate Conception Church
Mass at 9:30 A.M.

Interment Holy Cross Cemetery
Section Immaculta — Lot 22

LET US PRAY

O GENTLEST Heart of Jesus, ever present in the Blessed Sacrament, ever consumed with burning love for the poor captive souls in Purgatory have mercy on the soul of Thy departed servant. Be not severe in Thy judgment but let some drops of Thy Precious Blood fall upon the devouring flames, and do Thou O merciful Savior send Thy angels to conduct Thy departed servant to a place of refreshment, light and peace. Amen.

May the souls of all the faithful departed through the mercy of God, rest in peace. Amen.

SADOWSKI FUNERAL HOME

Spectacular
ICE SHOWS in the
Boulevard Room
THE STEVENS
CHICAGO

A joyous event of 1951 was the 40th wedding anniversary of Mike and Julia Madura. They celebrated with their three children and their spouses on September 11, 1951, at the Boulevard Room of the new Conrad Hilton Hotel in Chicago. The Boulevard Room featured spectacular ice-skating shows for an entertainment charge of $2, and their most expensive entrees (a la carte) of grilled prime aged sirloin steak or broiled live lobster with drawn butter were available for $6. From left to right are Michael and Evelyn (Madura) Halik, Mick and Henrietta Madura, Julia and Mike Madura, and Doris (Madura) and Arthur Borg.

Let's Go Dancing at Madura's

THE MAN WHO SUCCEEDED FRANK SINATRA WITH T. D.

When Frank Sinatra quit Tommy Dorsey a fellow named Allen DeWitt was called upon to fill Frankie's shoes. "Things were going great," says DeWitt, "playing all the bright spots and making recordings. Then Uncle Sam reached out and before long I was Sgt. DeWitt. We organized a big Army band which gave me the bug to have my own orchestra when I got out.

Instead, I rejoined Jan Savitt. Then Tiny Hill, Wayne King and recently Frankie Masters. Now, I've got what I always wanted—my own band. We just got to make good.

Madura's Danceland
INDIANAPOLIS BLVD. L CALUMET AVE.
FAMOUS 5 POINTS, HAMMOND, IND.

New Year's Eve 1953 featured the dueling bands of Allen DeWitt and Johnny Kay. DeWitt was Frank Sinatra's replacement in the Tommy Dorsey band before the war, and he later worked with Tiny Hill, Wayne King, and Frankie Masters before starting his own band. Other appearances during the 1950s and 1960s included Hoagy Carmichael, Russ Carlyle with singer Dorothy Ferguson, Tommy Allen, Don Baker, Billy Baxter, Ivar Buerk, Norm Carl, Phillip Carl, Dick Carlson, Jimmy Day, Pat DeMure, Johnny Edwards, Jimmy Featherstone, Mike Golden, Jerry Fifer, Eddie James, George Jessel, Ralph Marterie, Jim McHugh, Carl Mottinger, Frank Nachman, Bud Pressner, Jimmy Ray, Paul Rich, Al Stanley, Stardusters, Chester Steffen, Michael Stevens, Stanley Strug, Gene Victor, Craig Williams, Eddy Wilson, Frank Yankovic, Reynold Young, and Joe Zeglin.

Many high school proms were held at Danceland during the 1950s and 1960s. Pictured here are Marcia Madura and Daniel Kozlowski dancing at the George Rogers Clark High School prom of 1960.

The last of the big name bands to appear at Danceland was Guy Lombardo in November 1964. Guy Lombardo and the Royal Canadians sold more than 200 million records and had more than 500 hit tunes, and their popularity kept the band at New York City's Roosevelt Grill for 33 years. Every New Year's Eve they were broadcast over NBC-TV. They played for several presidential inaugurations and celebrities and were the favorite orchestra of Louis Armstrong. He claimed that they inspired him to record "Among My Souvenirs" and "Sweethearts on Parade." Unfortunately for the Maduras, the big band era had wound down, and even an admission charge of $5 for the 336 dancers who attended was not enough to cover the $1,750 cost of the band. A highly anticipated night was a disappointment and loss. The pictured window card was badly scorched in the Danceland fire of 1967.

By the mid-1950s, the big bands were no longer drawing the crowds they used to, and the few big ballrooms that survived the Depression were beginning to close. By the late 1940s and early 1950s, television was the new attraction and instead of going down to Madura's Danceland for a good time, people sat in their living rooms and watched the new *Lucille Ball Show* or the *Milton Berle Show*. Mike went back to ironworking to supplement his income. Danceland needed something new to sustain itself. Mick suggested the sale of alcohol, but his father would not hear of it. Perhaps it was his age—he was 68—or maybe his health. Mike Madura suffered a sudden heart attack and died on November 20, 1956. It was the end of an era and the end of his life.

Eight

THE ROCK-AND-ROLL ERA

The tide turned in 1960. After Mike's death, his widow, Julia, struggled for three years to make Danceland profitable but closed the ballroom during Lent and for three months in 1959 due to a lack of business. She then sold Danceland to her son Mick and Henrietta Madura for "one dollar and love and affection" on December 5, 1959.

When Mick took over the business, he continued featuring big band dances and renting the ballroom out for private dances, but he also had an elaborate fountain installed in the middle of the dance floor with tables around the rim of the floor to accommodate private parties. He even relaxed the 30-year-old dress code and allowed short-sleeve shirts.

But Elvis Presley had released his first album in 1956, and there was no turning back. Though wary of how rock-and-roll music would go over on a waltz and fox trot floor, Mick Madura watched the ballroom came alive again, with the offspring of the couples who met and married there in the 1930s and 1940s. The same rules applied—no liquor on the premises—and the dance floor, aisles, and restrooms were constantly patrolled. The hours of operation were from 7:00 p.m. to 10:00 p.m. The early popular dances were the bunny hop, the hokey pokey, and the Mexican hat dance, but later dances created by the teenagers included the bird, the watusi, and the roach. It was definitely a new era for "Madura's," as the teenagers preferred to call the ballroom, leaving the old moniker of "Danceland" for the old-timers to use.

After 67-year old Julia Madura (above) sold Danceland to Mick and Henrietta, they looked for new ways to bring the ballroom back to life. They found a perfect match in the 400 Club. Its president was Hobie Owen, its dance director was Andy Satanek, and its purpose was to promote the refinement of dance styles such as the foxtrot, cha-cha, jitterbug, and waltz. The original 400 Club was inspired by the National Ballroom Operator's Association, and Madura's 400 Club was started on November 3, 1961. It met on the first Friday of every month for over five years. Annual membership for couples was $40, and the club was limited to 200 couples.

"400 Dance Club"	PRINT NAME and ADDRESS clearly for our files
◆— Madura's Danceland —◆	
Whiting, Indiana	
Nº 63	
FIRST FRIDAY EACH MONTH	
1966 - 1967	
May 5☐ Sept. 2☐ Jan. 6☐ June 3☐	
Oct. 7☐ Feb. 3☐ July 1☐ Nov. 4☐	
Mar. 3☐ Aug. 5☐ Dec. 2☐ April 7☐	
Music by: Reynold Young	Nº 63

The Lake County
Democratic Central
Committee held its first
inaugural ball at Madura's
Danceland on December
27, 1962, attracting over
1,000 persons. The highlight
of the affair was the
inauguration of county and
township officials-elect. The
honored guest list included
Gov. Matthew Welsh and
U.S. senator-elect Birch
Bayh. Two years later, on
December 29, 1964, another
Democratic inaugural ball
was held, honoring Gov.
Roger Branigin, Gary
mayor A. Martin Katz,
and party chairman John
Krupa, who are pictured
at the head table on the
stage at Danceland (right).
Mike Kampo received the
Hammond Precinct Award
at that event (below).
(Photographs courtesy of
Stephen G. McShane.)

MADURA'S DANCELAND

WHITING, INDIANA
659-3114

CONTRACT FORM

Under the following terms and conditions of this contract it is understood that MADURA'S DANCELAND ballroom and accommodations be rendered to THE *REPUBLICAN Party* for the purpose of holding a ( ) semi-public ( ) private *CABARET STYLE* dance.

Date(s) of dance *SAT. NOV 5 1966* between basic (4) hours of *9 - 1*

BASIC PRICE AGREEMENT: $ *125.00* for up to *300* people $ ....

$ *85.00* for each additional *100* people $ ....

Final approximation will be made on day before dance.
PLEASE CALL You will be charged accordingly. $ ....

$ .... per hour for each P.M. (earlier) hour .... ( ) $ ....

$ *25.00* per ½ hour for each A.M. (overtime) hour .... ( ) $ ....
IF DESIRED

EXTRA ACCOMMODATIONS

( ) If Punch or other refreshments are brought in. $ ....

( ) If decorating or rehearsing takes place on day before dance. $ ....

( ) If extra band is used on north stage. $ ....

Total $ ....

MADURA'S DANCELAND shall operate checkroom and refreshment concessions, open ballroom half-hour before contract starting time; set up and take down own table and chair equipment.

The *REPUBLICANs* will hire union orchestra, (Name *DYNAMICS*) and permit no other entertainment without approval of ballroom management. *FREE IN*

1. Pay also all other expenses incurred by them, including (✓) police, advertising, tickets, and any breakage or loss to ballroom equipment.

2. a. Admit couples only, and whose dress, dancing and conduct conform with regular rules of this ballroom. b. Issue no pass-outs. c. Supply own door committee.

3. Forbid anyone from bringing outside mix (soft drinks and ice) on these premises. Such wordage to be printed on dance tickets.

4. To avoid overtime, band will quit playing at fulfillment of this contract, and committee official will stay until after dance urging crowd not to overstay their time, thus hindering employees in their expediency in complete clean-up as directed by City of Hammond Fire and Health Depts.

Added provisions *PATRONS SHOULD BRING THEIR OWN LIQUOR*

EXECUTED THIS *18* DAY OF *Aug* 19 *66*

$ .... held in escrow in case of damage or loss to ballroom property.

Accepted *Willard L. Owen*
Agent must be legal age of 21

Address *712 Southeastern Ave.*

Phone *Hammond 71-5-1523*

.... Madura's Danceland Official

The Republican Party rented the ballroom for a cabaret-style dance featuring music by the Dynamics on November 5, 1966. Willard L. Owen of Hammond signed the Danceland contract.

Television and radio star Fran Allison and Bishop Andrew Grutka enjoy a conversation on stage at a fund-raiser for Easter Seals in March 1967. Fran Allison was best known for her roles on the NBC puppet show *Kukla, Fran, and Ollie*, which ran from 1947 to 1957, and *The Breakfast Club*, a popular radio program from 1933 to 1968. Andrew Grutka was bishop of the Gary Diocese from 1956 to 1984.

Danceland was a wonderful place to hold lavish family wedding receptions. On November 4, 1961, Mick and Henrietta's son Michael D. married Charlene Dutko. On June 27, 1964, their oldest daughter, Marcia, married Daniel Kozlowski. The photograph above shows the grand march of 400 guests led by the bride and groom (Marcia and Daniel). This was traditionally followed by the receiving line, the garter throw, and the bouquet toss. At right, the band played and the guests sang "Let Me Call You Sweetheart" as Michael swept up his new bride, Charlene, and carried her out of Danceland to their honeymoon.

Ownership of Danceland had its joys and headaches. Besides the many pleasures, all family members had assigned jobs that were appropriate to their age and skills. While some jobs involved making good tips or meeting interesting people, others were less glamorous. For 38 years, the Maduras sold tickets, checked coats, served refreshments, prepared publicity, booked bands, set up party favors, ground and scattered paraffin floor wax, managed the books, painted the pickets, directed parking, hand-washed and dried glassware, cleaned out furnaces, and more. An old adding machine (above) and letterpress print blocks (below) used over the years are shown here.

Rock-and-roll "Record Hops" started at Danceland on January 8, 1960, with Jim Lounsbury as the emcee who played records. Lounsbury had been the host of *Bandstand Matinee* on WGN-TV, and in 1956 he staged his first of more than 2,000 Record Hops at ballrooms in Illinois, Indiana, Wisconsin, and Michigan. The musicians' union frowned on the lack of live musicians hired for this venture, yet most of the union musicians were unfamiliar with the new music. Lounsbury proceeded to hire four young roll-and-roll musicians per show, which was the beginning of live rock music in Chicago. His television show *Record Hop* was broadcast right before Dick Clark's *American Bandstand* on ABC-TV.

The November 4, 1957, edition of *Time* magazine stated, "Rock music is here to stay." And so the Record Hops put "Madura's" on the map again. Popular DJs were Ralph Cox, Jan Gabriel, Dick Biondi, Bob Hale, Jack Hilton, and Art Roberts. Roberts (pictured) was Chicago's famed WLS disc jockey and is remembered by one fan for handing out free 45-inch records of "Every Day and Every Night" by the Trolls, who appeared in October 1966. Roberts commented that he "had many appearances at Madura's Danceland and always enjoyed performing before a very enthusiastic crowd. The old ballrooms of yesterday each have a history, and most of them date back to the big bands. Too bad we don't have treasures like that to share today." The last four years of Danceland Record Hops were held on Sundays, and Tony Powell booked the bands.

One of the earliest bands was Jimmy and the Jeepers from northwest Indiana, which was an immediate hit at Danceland. The band included Jimmy McHugh, Paul Wojtena, Norbie King, and Willy Henson. Gary and the Knight-Lites (pictured) were another favorite and later made the hit record "Bend Me, Shape Me" under their new name, The American Breed.

Singer Lou Christie's characteristic sound was his controlled high falsetto. Appearing at Danceland on June 13, 1963, Christie had two new hit singles, "The Gypsy Cried" and "Two Faces Have I." Lou Christie recorded another big hit in 1966, "Lightnin' Strikes," which hinted at the fate of Danceland. Pictured here, Lou Christie is rehearsing on the Danceland main stage.

Conway Twitty (left) appeared at Madura's Danceland on November 24, 1963, with his hits "It's Only Make Believe" (1958) and "Lonely Blue Boy." That same year, Danceland featured another teen idol, Johnny Tillotson (below), whose "Poetry in Motion" (1960) with Floyd Cramer on piano and Boots Randolph on saxophone reached no. 2 in the United States and no. 1 one in the United Kingdom. Bobby Vee also appeared and had several hits, including "Take Good Care of My Baby" (1961), "Run to Him" (1961), "Roses Are Red, My Love" (1962), and "The Night Has a Thousand Eyes," which reached no. 3 on the U.S. charts.

Others stars included Jimmy Gilmer (right) and the Fireballs, who appeared at Madura's Danceland on March 22, 1964, with their chart-toppers "Sugar Shack" and "Suzie Q." Bobby Goldsboro (below) appeared on May 10, 1964, with the first of a string of top-40 hits and his own composition, "See the Funny Little Clown." Later hits included "Honey," "Watching Scotty Grow," and "Little Green Apples." Earlier in his career he worked as Roy Orbison's guitarist, and he also helped produce the group The Boys Next Door. Guitarist Webb Foley, whose style ranged from Elvis Presley to Johnny Cash, also played at Danceland.

The Kingsmen's recording of "Louie Louie" (1963) rose to no. 2 on the charts and influenced countless other bands with its raucous melody and simple harmonies. Although the tune was banned in Indiana for alleged obscene lyrics, the band played it at Danceland on February 16, 1964, and was led by singer Lynn Easton (above). Other mainstream groups with an added bit of novelty included Sam the Sham and the Pharaohs (below) on October 3, 1965, with their garage-band classic hits "Wooly Bully" (1965) and "Lil' Red Riding Hood" (1966) and Cannibal and the Headhunters, who appeared three weeks later with their rock hit "Land of 1,000 Dances."

Some of the purely instrumental groups were Johnny and the Hurricanes (right), who featured the guitar on "Crossfire" (1959) and saxophone and organ on "Red River Rock," "Reveille Rock," "Beatnik Fly," "Down Yonder," and "Ja-Da." The Bill Black Combo (below) featured the piano on "White Silver Sands" (1962), which reached no. 9 on the U.S. charts. Bill Black was a bass player for Elvis Presley in his early years, and he formed his own band in 1959, including Carl McAvoy on piano, Reggie Young on guitar, Martin Will on saxophone, and Jerry Arnold on drums. The group had a total of 19 U.S. chart singles.

Surf and folk-rock groups were also popular at Danceland. The Rivieras (pictured), a five-piece group (guitar, organ, bass, drums, and voice) from South Bend, Indiana, made a no. 5 hit with their "California Sun" in 1964. The folk-rock group The Critters is best remembered for "Mr. Dieingly Sad" and "Don't Let the Rain Fall Down on Me."

JAY and THE AMERICANS

Rock groups began to experiment in the mid-1960s and featured more advanced musical materials than found in early rock-and-roll. One of Danceland's best performances was by Jay and the Americans on Valentine's Day, 1965, featuring their 1964 hits "Come a Little Bit Closer" and "Let's Lock the Door."

Other popular rock-group appearances were by The Guess Who, led by Chad Allan (right), on November, 21, 1965; the vocal quartet The Vogues (below) on January 16, 1966, with their 1965 hit "Five O'Clock World"; Chicago group the New Colony Six on January, 30, 1966, with their hit of that year "I Confess"; The Buckinghams in April and June of 1966 with their hit "Kind of a Drag"; the Cryan' Shames with "Sugar and Spice"; and the Blues Magoos on November 24, 1966, with their hit of that year, "We Ain't Got Nothin' Yet" from their *Psychedelic Lollipop* album.

Other rock groups that performed at Madura's Danceland were Mousie and the Traps (above), The Exceptions (left), The Apollos, Barons, Bazooties, Blue Angels, Capitols, Classic Five, Continentals, Crestons, Delites, Delvets, Destination, Diplomats, Exports, Five Bucks, Fugitives, Roy Head, Jaguars, Jokers, Jordans, Kritters, Little Boy Blues, Little Kings, Majestics, Michael and the Messengers, Mob, Mystics, Pride and Joy, Powder Puffs, Proper Strangers, Princetons, Ravelles, Ravens, Rogues, Rovin' Kind, Saturday's Children, Seagrams, Shadows of Night, Still Life, Things to Come, Trade Winds, Vice Roys, Vikings, What For, and The Young Gentlemen. Prophetically, The Omens were the last group to play at Danceland before its devastating fire.

Two favorite groups appearing at Madura's in the late 1960s were The Boys Next Door (right) and The Still Life (below). The Boys Next Door, from Indianapolis, were considered The Beach Boys of the Midwest and issued hits in "Mandy," "She'd Rather Be with Me," and "See the Way She's Mine." The band members autographed these photographs for 13-year-old Patrice Madura, the youngest of the Madura siblings and cousins. Although she was a classical pianist and organist by this time, her great enthusiasm for the new rock-and-roll music perhaps balanced her father's deep nostalgia for the big band era.

The Boys Next Door

The Wilshires was a favorite band that played at Madura's Danceland seven times in 1966 and 1967. The members were (first row, kneeling) John Hulick and (second row, left to right) Donny Marovich, Ed Salerno, Herbie Hagenwald, and John Higgerson. The group played the songs of the Turtles, Vanilla Fudge, The Young Rascals, The Beach Boys, and Donovan. John Higgerson, who played bass guitar with the Wilshires from 1966 to 1968 and later went on to record a hit album with the group Trouble, reminisced, "We were trying to be like The Beatles." Higgerson was 16 years old when he began playing with The Wilshires and recalled that as a member of Musicians Local Union 203, the band was paid approximately $375 to $425 a night. According to Higgerson, "You had arrived when you got to play at Madura's!"

Nine

ALL GOOD THINGS MUST COME TO AN END

It was Sunday morning, July 23, 1967, and the Madura family was attending Mass at Sacred Heart Church in Whiting. They looked forward to celebrating Henrietta's 54th birthday later that afternoon. Daughter Patrice, age 15, was the church organist on that day, and after descending the pipe organ loft, she was told that her parents had been rushed out of church by cousin Patti Halik because their "house" was burning down. Patrice asked the Fortins, friends of the family, to drive her home, and they found the family home still standing, with no sign of fire. However, they then saw a huge, billowing, black cloud of smoke in the sky in the direction of Danceland, about a half-mile away. Fire trucks had Five Points blocked in every direction, and the all-wooden structure burned completely to the ground while the Madura family and dozens of others watched in horror and disbelief.

Son Michael D. (Mickey), Charlene, and children Michele (age 4) and Michael A. (age 2) were driving from Hammond to Whiting for Henrietta's birthday celebration when they saw the black smoke in the distance. When Mickey identified himself, the firemen allowed him to drive through the blockade, and his family watched Danceland burn. Daughter Marcia and husband Dan were living in Indianapolis when they received the phone call about the fire, but were told, "Don't rush—it's too late—it has burned down." During the three-hour drive to Whiting, Marcia just couldn't imagine what she would say to her father. When she got to the house, he appeared calm and philosophical. He said, "The important thing is that we are all still alive, and that this didn't happen during a dance. Not one person died."

Danceland business had been good in recent years for the Maduras, and Mick had made many physical improvements to his ballroom (above). That Sunday, July 23, 1967, was going to be a special day to relax and celebrate Henrietta's birthday. While Mick was shaving that morning, he heard a loud crack of thunder and thought to himself, "That was close," not knowing how close it really was. Mick, Henrietta, and Patrice attended Sacred Heart Church (below) that morning, the same church where Mike and Julia Madura were married in 1911 and where their children and grandchildren married. On that fateful morning, a lightning bolt struck Madura's Danceland.

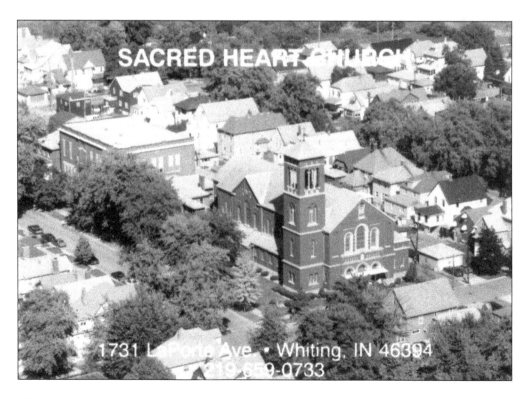

Mick Madura (seen here) raced out of church and drove the mile to Danceland, where he watched his ballroom burn to the ground. He later wrote, "Though the grand old dame was alone when lightning struck her backbone, many had gathered tearfully by the roadside as her melody-soaked arches fell burning across the dance floor. What they remembered as a scene of happy faces, now were seen as a sea of flames—flames dancing with the devil making a macabre mockery. What was so often a sea of dreamy dances, this once-famous spring cushion dance floor now was a sea of nightmarish flames. Though she loved company, she knew when she was ripped by the slash of lightning, it would be better to be alone when her time was up. No fanfare, no headlines. She just faded away to ashes as quickly as fate intended."

The Hammond Fire Department arrived at the site shortly before noon and fought the inferno. They reported that flames shot out of the doors and windows when they were broken open, and that the domed roof crashed down within minutes. The Maduras watched helplessly from the Five Points intersection, which the police had closed to traffic. The fire department said that lightning struck the utility pole near the fuse box backstage, and it certainly struck the family's soul. The mammoth wooden arches, magnificent chandeliers, two stages with their respective grand pianos, and the famous maple wood dance floor were all burned rubble in just a few hours. Hearts broke with every falling beam.

A fan wrote, "Some of my happiest times were the many evenings spent dancing and listening to the great bands there. I, like so many others, met my wife on that dance floor. On the morning of the fire, when the first sirens sounded on Calumet Avenue, I looked out and saw the rising smoke but didn't know where the fire was located. I grabbed my camera and got to the fire early. I was able to capture some pictures before the whole building became engulfed in flames. What a sad and depressing sight! So many wonderful memories slowly floated away in the dark, black smoke." (Courtesy of George W. Girman.)

One of the saddest sights was the burned Steinway grand piano, at left, in a heap of rubble under a fallen beam. Below, Henrietta Madura stands under the ruins of the massive ballroom arch wondering how the family would move forward. Nothing remained except for some glassware, a bible, and band poster ads with burned edges. The contents of the building were not insured, and due to the recent fire at McCormick's Place in Chicago, their building insurance would barely cover the removal of the wreckage. She wondered how they would pay for Patrice's college education and if Mick would need to find a new job after 38 years at Danceland.

Mick Madura stands by the destroyed cooling system he had recently purchased (right). He had also replaced the sidewalk and the roof that year at a cost of $40,000, and they were not paid for yet. Danceland had been Mick's work and joy for his whole life, and he felt lost when it no longer existed. He spent his days tending the land where Danceland had stood. He let the trees and bushes grow, he grew watermelons, and he built a gazebo (below) out of marble sections of a dismantled communion rail from Sacred Heart Church. The city eventually forced him to clear the land, and he accepted an offer from a fan to buy what was left of the famous maple wood dance floor to build a cabin in Cedar Lake, Indiana.

Mick considered rebuilding, but starting over as he approached the age of 60 was overwhelming. He decorated a room with Danceland posters that survived the fire with burned edges, listened to big band records, wrote nostalgic memoirs, and participated in radio and newspaper interviews (above). Mick and Henrietta (below) lived for two years on their savings, but then they found work in Chicago, where Henrietta stayed employed by Time-Life for 10 years. On January 16, 1980, over 12 years after the fire, Mick sold the land that he loved for $90,000 to a Car-X Auto Service franchise. Shortly thereafter, he succumbed to lung cancer and died on July 31, 1984, at the age of 72. Henrietta lived for another 20 years, enjoying the fruits of the business and nine great-grandchildren that Mick never saw, including one more Michael (N.) Madura.

Madura's Danceland was brought to life again on May 18, 2003, when the newest South Shore Line poster, commissioned by Marcia and Daniel Kozlowski, was unveiled in a ceremony at the legendary Phil Smidt restaurant. Shown from left to right are (seated) Doris Madura Borg, Henrietta Madura, and Evelyn Madura Halik; (standing) Diane Borg Richardson, Patrice Madura Ward-Steinman, Marcia Madura Kozlowski, Michael D. Madura, and Bonnie Halik Kekelik.

It was as if Madura's Danceland had a soul. A risk-taking businessman and his artistic son gave Danceland life. For 38 years, people came to dance to the live music of the times, they fell in love, and they married. Danceland dominated the Madura family life and is their special legacy, and so its story is told to recreate the flavor of a time and place to be remembered.

BIBLIOGRAPHY

Bopp, Ron. *The American Carousel Organ: An Illustrated Encyclopedia.* St. Cloud: MN: Palmer Printing, 1998.

Bryant, Rebecca A. *Shaking Big Shoulders: Music and Dance Culture in Chicago, 1910–1925.* University of Illinois at Urbana-Champaign, 2003. (UMI Number: 3086023.)

Gault, Lon A. *Ballroom Echoes.* Andrew Corbet Press, 1989.

Korall, Bert. *Drummin' Men: The Heartbeat of Jazz, The Swing Years.* New York: Schirmer Books, 1990.

Lounsbury, Jim. *"Hey, Look, I'm on TV": Chicago Television and Rock N' Roll, The Early Years.* Tucson, AZ: Jim Lounsbury Enterprises, 2000.

McKinlay, Archibald. *Oil and Water: A Pictorial History of Whiting/Robertsdale, Indiana.* Virginia Beach, VA: The Donning Company Publishers, 2003.

Schoon, Kenneth J. *Calumet Beginnings: Ancient Shorelines and Settlements at the South End of Lake Michigan.* Bloomington, IN: Indiana University Press, 2003.

Schuller, Gunther. *The Swing Era.* New York: Oxford, 1989.

Sellers, Rod and Dominic Pacyga. *Chicago's Southeast Side.* Chicago: Arcadia Publishing, 1998.

Sengstock, Charles, A., Jr. *That Toddlin' Town: Chicago's White Dance Bands and Orchestras, 1900–1950.* Champaign, IL: University of Illinois Press, 2004.

Spink, Al. *Spink Sport Stories: 1000 Big and Little Ones* (volume 2). Chicago: The Martin Company, 1921.

Stockdale, Robert, L. *Jimmy Dorsey: A Study in Contrasts.* Lanham, MD: Scarecrow Press, 1999.

Wald, Elijah (2007). "Louis Armstrong loves Guy Lombardo!: Acknowledging the Smoother Roots of Jazz." *Jazz Research Journal*, 1(1), 129–145.

Walker, Leo. *The Wonderful Era of the Great Dance Bands.* Garden City: NY: Doubleday, 1972.

INDEX

Visit us at
arcadiapublishing.com